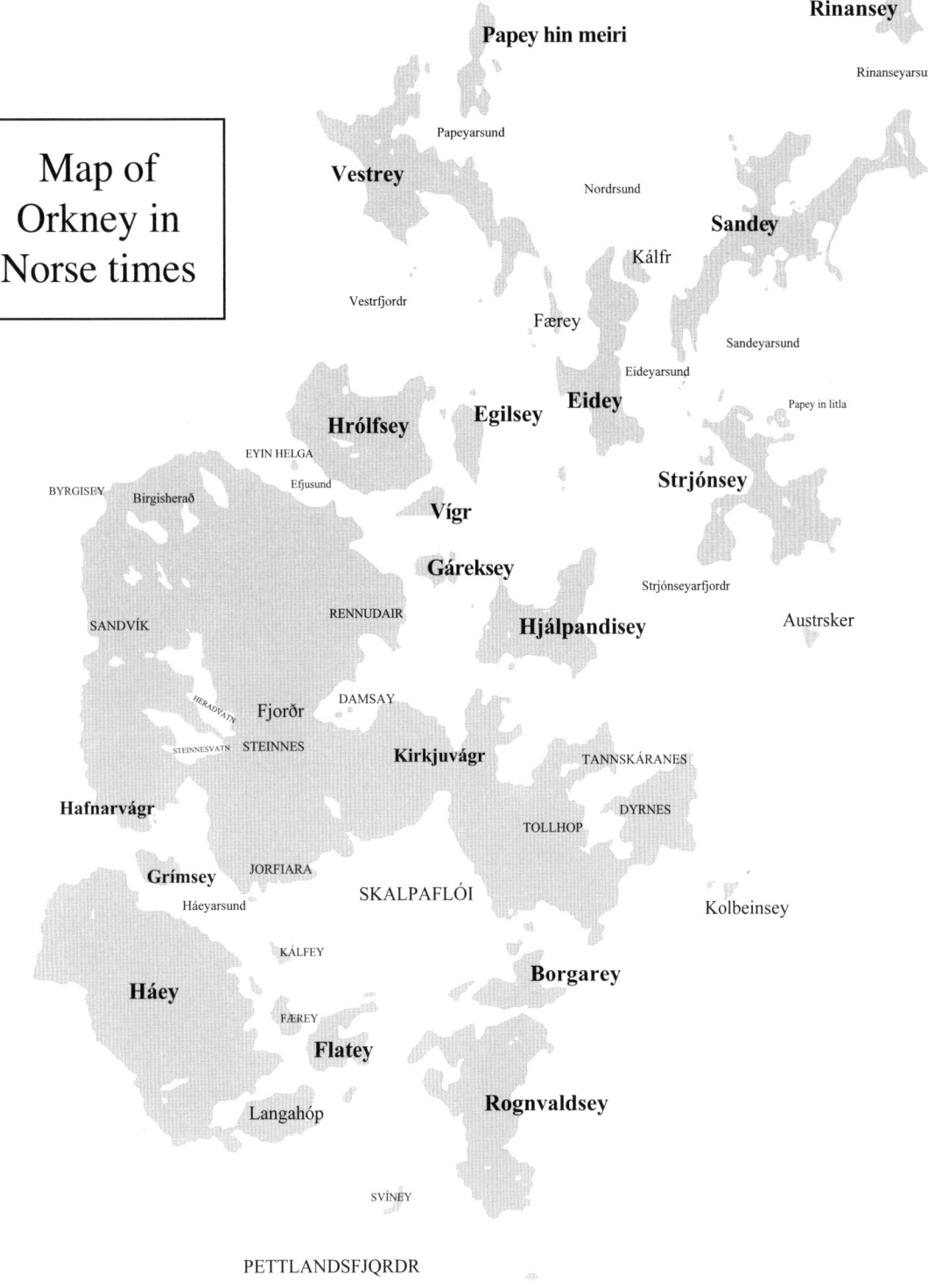

ORKNEY IN THE SAGAS

The Story of the Earldom of Orkney
as told in the Icelandic Sagas

by
Tom Muir

With additional articles by
Barbara E Crawford
Anne Brundle
Julie Gibson
Steven P Ashby

Edited by
Steve Callaghan

A page from Orkneyinga Saga contained in the Saga of St Olaf in the Flateyjarbok. It starts with the sentence 'King Olaf Haraldsson did not get any taxes from earl Thorfinn'. – The University of Iceland

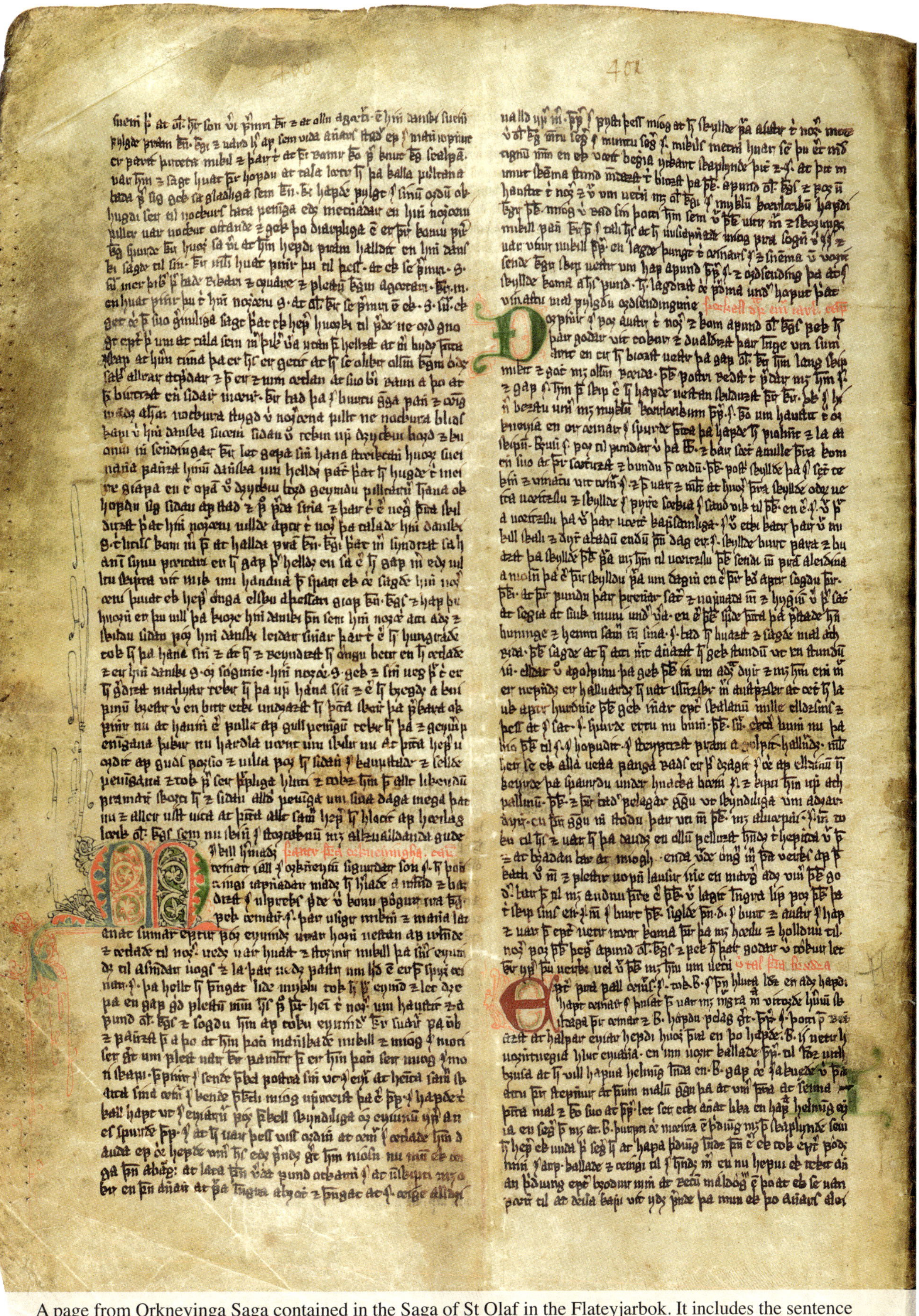

A page from Orkneyinga Saga contained in the Saga of St Olaf in the Flateyjarbok. It includes the sentence 'A great soldier Einar earl of Orkneyjar'. – The University of Iceland

DEDICATION

To all the people who have been involved in the Destination Viking – Sagalands project

ACKNOWLEDGEMENTS

Tom Muir is Exhibitions Officer with Orkney Museums and Heritage and a noted and well-travelled storyteller.

Dr Barbara Crawford is a medieval historian, and Director of the Strathmartine Centre in St Andrews.

Anne Brundle is Curator of Archaeology with Orkney Museums and Heritage and a research student at the University of York.

Julie Gibson is County Archaeologist, employed by Orkney Archaeological Trust, and lectures at Orkney College.

Steve Ashby is a research student at the University of York, studying the production, use and role of combs in medieval Northern Europe.

Steve Callaghan is head of service for Orkney Museums and Heritage, part of Orkney Islands Council.

Special thanks to Babette Berthelmess and Bryce Wilson for their help and constructive suggestions and to Raymond Parks for his generous gift of photographs for this publication

Cover photograph – Scar Plaque, Scar Boat Burial, Sanday – Rik Hammond

All photographs of sites managed by Historic Scotland were taken with the permission of site staff.

Every effort has been made to establish copyright of images used in this publication.
Anyone with a query or possible claim in this regard should contact Orkney Islands Council in the first instance.

Printed and Published at The Orcadian Limited, Hatston, Kirkwall, Orkney

Orkney in the Sagas – The story of the Earldom of Orkney as told in the Icelandic Sagas
First edition published in 2005

Hardback ISBN 0-9548862-2-4 – Paperback ISBN 0-9548862-3-2

CONTENTS

	Page No.
Map of Orkney in Norse Times	
Dedication	
Acknowledgements	
Contents	
The Earls of Orkney	
Introduction	
Of Gods and Earls: Mythological Beginnings	1
King Harald Fair-Hair and the Early Earls of Orkney	3
Viking Graves – Anne Brundle	10/11
Scar Boat Burial – Anne Brundle	12-14
Turf Einar and the Sons of King Harald	15
Birsay: the Brough and Village – Julie Gibson	22-25
Sigurd the Stout and the Raven Banner	27
Westness, Rousay – Julie Gibson	38-41
Earl Thorfinn the Mighty	43
Brough of Deerness – Julie Gibson	56/57
Saint Magnus	59
Ships – Anne Brundle	68/69
The Miracles of St Magnus	71
Kirkwall – Julie Gibson	74/75
Rognvald Kali Becomes Earl	77
Earl Rognvald's Pilgrimage – Barbara E Crawford	84-86
The Adventures of Earl Rognvald	87
Hoards – Anne Brundle	94/95
The War of the Three Earls	97
Orphir – Julie Gibson	104/105
The Death of Svein Asleifsson	107
Horses – Anne Brundle	110/111
Earl Harald Maddadsson and the Loss of Shetland	113
Westray – Julie Gibson	120/121
King Hakon Hakonsson, the Last of the Great Sea-kings	123
Combs – Steven P Ashby	134/136
Runes – Steve Callaghan	138/139
Saga Translations Used in this Book	141
Map of Orkney in Modern Times	143

THE EARLS OF OF ORKNEY

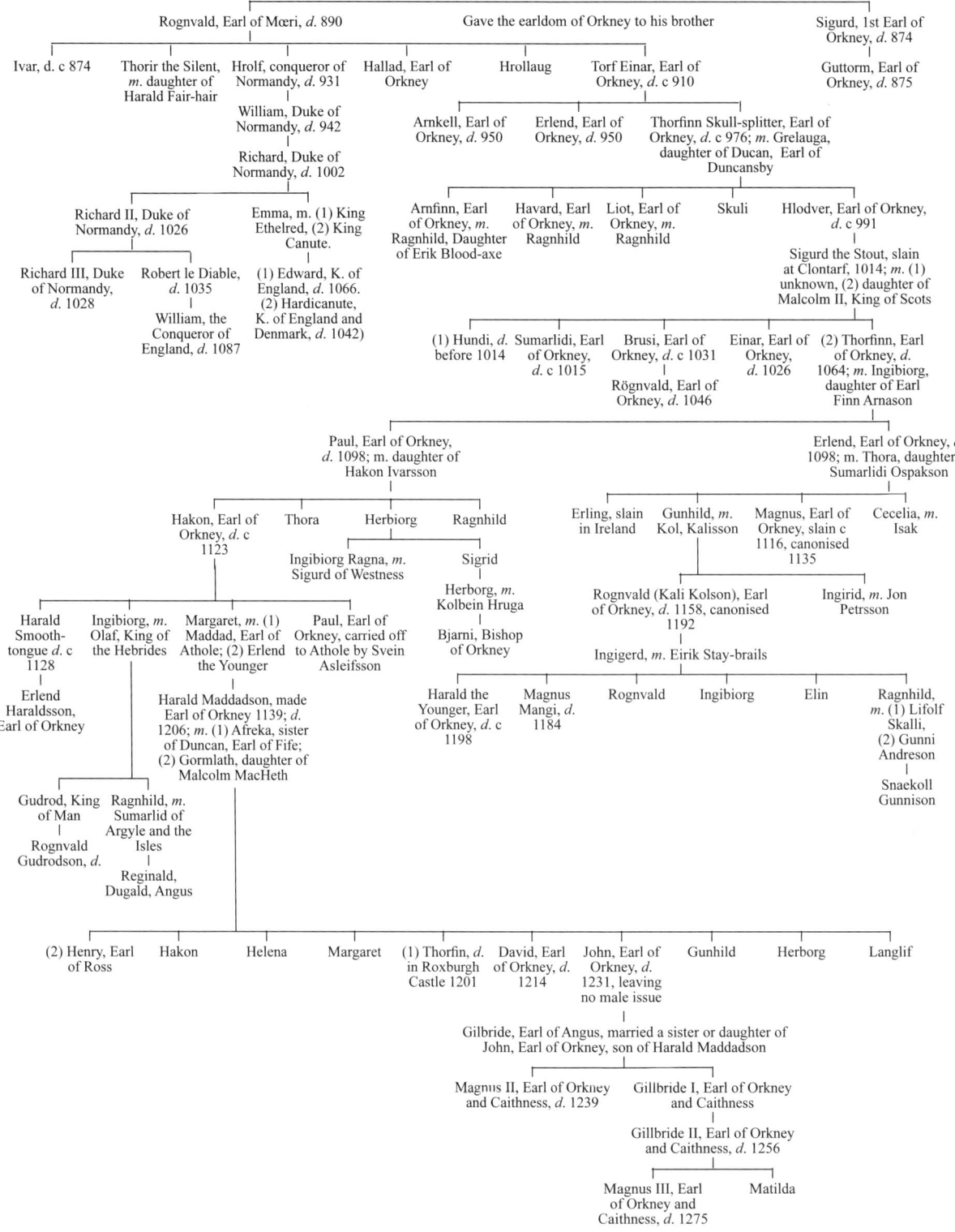

INTRODUCTION

Orkney is said to have come under the control of the king of Norway around the year 874, although Scandinavian people had started to settle in the islands from the late eighth century. It was in 874 that King Harald Fair-hair seized power in a series of battles against his fellow regional kings, uniting Norway under his rule. Many people were driven from Norway and settled in other countries, like Iceland. Others became Vikings, which actually means pirates who would raid settlements and churches and carry off people to be sold as slaves. The term Viking has since come to include everyone in Scandinavia from the late eighth century to the late eleventh centuries, even if they were farmers and traders who had never been on a raid in their lives.

It was in Iceland that the stories of great warriors, poets, outlaws, kings and earls were told by the fireside during the long winter nights. Icelanders are fiercely proud of their heritage, and from the thirteenth century these tales were written down in books that are known as the Icelandic Sagas. Many have been lost; some were even eaten during times of famine when the calf skins that the sagas were written on became more valuable as food than the stories they recorded.

The sagas are no-nonsense accounts of family feuds, battles, law-suits and honour. A man's reputation was worth more than gold, and a death left unavenged was a stain on his character. Great events were recorded in the sagas, like the discovery of Greenland and North America by the Vikings, many centuries before Columbus discovered the West Indies. The sagas of the kings of Norway were recorded by Snorri Sturluson (*c.*1179–1241) at his home of Reykholt, and are still available to this day in a book called *Heimskringla*. It may have been Snorri who wrote the wonderfully dramatic *Egil's Saga*, set around the beautiful Borgarnes region of western Iceland. We don't know the authors of other epics like *Njal's Saga* and *Laxdæla Saga*, but they remain as vivid and exciting to modern readers as they would have done to medieval Icelanders.

Orkney is very lucky, as it has its own saga that tells the history of the earls of Orkney over a period of more than three centuries. The original, called the *Jarlasaga* (the saga of the earls), was a collection of histories of the early earls of Orkney. This prototype, together with other now lost sagas, was used to produce the longer and more up-to-date *Orkneyinga Saga* (the saga of the Orkney islanders) around the year 1200. This version also recorded the history of Earl Rognvald Kali, his friend and sometimes foe, Svein Asleifsson, and Earl Harald Maddadsson. It is likely that the finishing touches were added to it later in the thirteenth century, possibly in 1234–35, when two leading Orcadians were staying in Iceland. One of them was a grandson of Svein Asleifsson, which may explain why his escapades feature so largely in the saga. Snorri knew the earlier version of the *Jarlasaga*, and he used it while he was compiling *Heimskringla*. We find a whole potted version of the saga in one section of Snorri's classic history, ending at the time of Earl Thorfinn the Mighty.

Who the writer of the *Orkneyinga Saga* was, we simply don't know. What we do know is that the book was copied several times, which may have led to some revision of the text. The beginning of the saga is a mythological tale about the ancestors of the earls of Orkney. This is similar in style to the introduction of Snorri's *Heimskringla,* but who influenced whom? What is sure is that the *Orkneyinga Saga* is a fascinating book, full of twists and turns. It lifts the curtain of history to give the reader a glimpse into the world of the Vikings.

Orkney was a powerful place during the Viking period, lying at the crossroads between the Scandinavian and Celtic worlds. This can be seen by the frequent references to Orkney in the Icelandic Sagas. This book tries to pull together many of these strands to tell the story of these islands during this turbulent period of their history. The fact that so many sagas are referred to in this publication gives the reader some idea of just how important Orkney was to the Vikings and their descendants.

We must bear in mind that the sagas are literary works, and not an accurate historical record. Also, some sagas have their own agenda, depending upon who was paying for them. A saga writer was not going to give his client a critical write-up; the victories were played up while the defeats were glossed over. In the *Orkneyinga Saga* the writer depicts the earls of Orkney as rulers in their own right, only playing lip service to the king of Norway. In Snorri's *Heimskringla* the earls are cast in a more subservient role, and the Norwegian kings portrayed as all-powerful. As long as we remember that we are reading works of literature based on real historical characters (and indeed, sometimes not even that), we should be alright. The nearer to our own time the more accurate they become, as the events were still fresh in people's memory. To deliberately lie about an event would make the supposed hero look ridiculous, much to the detriment of his character. So, enjoy the sagas and go and explore them. As you can see from this book, the Viking history of the Orkney Islands does not stop with the *Orkneyinga Saga*.

Tom Muir

Reikholt Church and Saga Centre, built on the site of Snorri Sturluson's house – Tom Muir

OF GODS AND EARLS: MYTHOLOGICAL BEGINNINGS

This chapter gives an account of the mythological ancestors of the earls of More in Norway, from whom the earls of Orkney were descended. The saga writer wanted to make the bold statement that the earls of Orkney were in no way inferior to the kings of Norway.

The *Orkneyinga Saga* begins with a mythical account of the ancestors of the earls of Orkney. It says that King Fornjot ruled the northernmost part of Scandinavia in ancient times. He had three sons, Hler (also called Ægir), Logi and Kari. These three sons were in fact natural elements; water, fire and air. Ægir was a sea-god or sea-giant, Logi means 'flames', while Kari was a name for the north wind. Fornjot himself is listed in the great saga writer Snorri Sturluson's book *Prose Edda* as a giant; a creature synonymous with earth and rocks. Although Christian by the time that *Prose Edda* was written (c1220), Icelanders knew the tales of the Old Norse gods and the name of the giant would not have been lost on them.

Kari had a son called Frosti (frost), who had a son called Snær the Old ('snær' means 'snow' in Old Norse), whose son was Thorri (the dry one). Thorri had two sons, Nor and Gor, and a daughter called Goi. Thorri used to make sacrifices to the gods in midwinter, so much so that it was said that a winter month was named after him. During one of these sacrifices his daughter Goi disappeared and his two sons went in search of her. Nor searched the mainland using skis to travel over the snow, while Gor searched all the islands and outlying rocks in his ship. After a while the two brothers met and divided the land between them; Gor claimed the islands off Norway while Nor claimed the mainland, naming it Norway after himself. They both set off again in search of their sister. Nor eventually found her; she had been carried off by King Hrolf, the son of a giant called Svadi. They fought together in single combat for quite some time without either gaining the upper hand. Eventually they came to terms; Hrolf kept Goi as his wife while Nor married Hrolf's sister. Nor returned with his new wife to rule the kingdom he had claimed. Gor continued to rule all the islands off Norway and he came to be called a sea-king.

Gor had two sons, Heiti and Beiti, who were aggressive and warlike men. They attacked the kingdom of the sons of Nor who lived on the mainland. On one occasion they had a boat dragged over a neck of land, with Gor sitting in the stern with his hand on the tiller, and they claimed this as part of their sea-kingdom. It was from Heiti that Earl Rognvald of More in Norway was said to have been descended. Earl Rognvald of More was a powerful chieftain, and it was from him that the earls of Orkney were descended.

The four elements, fire, water, earth and air, were the mythical ancestors of the earls of More and Orkney, although the earth element was less significant. The fact that Fornjot was a giant was more important than the element he could be associated with. The others were synonymous with the harsh winter weather of the arctic north. Here the saga writer is making the point that these people were of the far north and that their ancestors were of supernatural origin. But why?

In Snorri Sturluson's epic *Heimskringla* (the sagas of the Kings of Norway), he begins with an account of the mythological origins of the kings of Scandinavia. It is said that Odin, accompanied by other gods, left Asgard in Asia and travelled northwards to settle in Sweden. Odin was a powerful sorcerer and a great leader in battle and ended up being worshiped as a god. It is likely that the Christian Snorri Sturluson couldn't claim that these people were indeed gods, but portrayed them as foreigners with magical powers who were accepted as gods. Many kings claimed descent from Odin. The later dynasty of the Norwegian kings was said to be descended from the god Frey, also known as Frey Yngvi. This dynasty was called the Ynglings. The mythical ancestors of the earls of Orkney, King Fornjot and his descendants, have no connection with these gods, and that was the very point that the saga writer was making. Although Nor was said to have been king of Norway, neither he nor his family had any connections with the later Yngling kings, descended from King Harald Fair-hair. Nor and his family were from the far north; their early ancestors were associated with extreme winter weather conditions and were of the race of giants. The Yngling kings claimed descent from the gods who had travelled north from Asia. They were from foreign lands far to the south, unlike the purely Norwegian earls. The fact that the earls claimed descent from a giant, the arch enemies of the gods, is also important. Here we have two sides that claim supernatural ancestry, but who are not connected. Thus, while the earls hold land from the king they are portrayed as being in no way inferior, and indeed more Norwegian than the kings of Norway.[1]

Ring of Brodgar, Stenness – Keith Allardyce

[1] Sorensen, Preben Meulengracht. 'The Legendary Ancestors of the Earls of Orkney', *The Viking Age in Caithness, Orkney and the North Atlantic.* Edinburgh University Press, 1993. 212–221.

KING HARALD FAIR-HAIR AND THE EARLY EARLS OF ORKNEY

The events in this chapter take place c874–c.894. At that time King Harald was the ruler of a small kingdom in Norway. He started a bloody war against the other regional kings until he became the only ruler of a united Norway. Powerful chieftains who had been driven from their lands left Norway and settled in Shetland, Orkney and the Hebrides, where they became Vikings – pirates who made a living from raiding. With Norway under attack from these Vikings, King Harald led an expedition west to bring these islands under his control. His right-hand-man, Earl Rognvald of More, was given Orkney and Shetland by King Harald, but he in turn gave the islands to his brother Sigurd, who became the first earl of Orkney.

Heimskringla tells us how King Harald Fair-hair seized power in Norway sometime around the year 874 and united the country under the rule of one king. He originally ruled a kingdom within Norway, basing himself in Trondheim, while other kings ruled their own lands throughout the country. King Harald had sent messengers to a young woman called Gyda, the daughter of King Erik of Hordaland, asking her to marry him. She refused, saying that when he could unite all of Norway under his own rule, like King Gorm in Denmark and King Erik in Sweden, then she would be his wife. The messengers returned to King Harald with that

Yesnaby – Raymond Parks

message, and they urged him to carry her off by force. King Harald refused, saying that she had spoken wisely and that such thoughts were already on his mind. He also made the vow that he would neither cut nor comb his hair until he was king of all Norway. He attacked the other kings, defeating them and putting earls in control of the lands with the power to raise taxes and to keep the law in the king's name.

When King Harald defeated the kings of North More and Romsdale he appointed Earl Rognvald the Mighty (also called Rognvald the Shrewd) as earl over these lands. Earl Rognvald became a powerful supporter of King Harald, and it was from him that the earls of Orkney were descended. Earl Rognvald would later add South More to his estate after King Harald defeated the rulers of that shire. The battles continued for years, while some of the regional kings submitted to King Harald and were put in charge as earls on his behalf. Others found the loss of face too much to bear and continued to raid King Harald's lands in Norway. These displaced chieftains stayed with the remaining kings who had not as yet been defeated. Some left Norway to settle overseas in Shetland, Orkney, the Hebrides, and as far as Iceland. With civil war raging in Norway, King Erik of Sweden invaded Varmland and West Gautland, setting an earl over this extension to his kingdom. This caused King Harald to lead his army through the disputed areas, calling the bonders (landowners) to an assembly and charging them with treason.

The kings of Hordaland and Rogaland in western Norway, Telemark in the east and Agder in the south joined forces to take on the might of King Harald. They met in a sea-battle at Hafrsfjord, to the west of the modern-day city of Stavanger, in the year 874. It was a huge

Wheems, South Ronaldsay – Raymond Parks

and bloody affair, which King Harald finally won. The last of the regional kings were killed, including King Erik of Hordaland, whose daughter Gyda has set this chain of events in motion. After that King Harald had total control over all of Norway. With his vow complete he had his hair cut and combed by Earl Rognvald of More while attending a feast at the earl's estate. The earl remarked that while he had been known as Harald Thick-hair before he should now be known as Harald Fair-hair, as his hair was so fine and beautiful.

Although Harald had been married and had several children he still called for Gyda to be brought to him. With his task complete she married him and they had five children. He then married Ragnhild the Mighty, who was the daughter of King Erik of Jutland. (It was said that Harald had already divorced nine previous wives by this time.) Harald and Ragnhild had a son called Erik Blood-axe. After Ragnhild's death King Harald went feasting one winter in Uplands. There he was approached by a Finn called Svasi (Finns were from the far north and were believed to have magical powers), and was invited to visit his hut. The king went with Svasi the Finn to his hut and there he met Snæfrid, the Finn's beautiful daughter. She handed him a cup of mead, which he drank, and then he took her by the hand. It was as if fire ran through his veins, and he said that he must lie with her that very night. Svasi refused, saying that he must marry her before he could have her. Harald was bewitched; he married Snæfrid immediately and loved her so much that he neglected his kingdom. Two of their sons were Halfdan Highleg and Gudrod Gleam who will come into the story later. Snæfrid died, but the colour of her skin never faded and she looked as if she was only asleep. For three years Harald sat by her bed in grief, before a wise counsellor suggested that they should lift her body and dress it in new clothes. As soon as they raised her body from the bed there came a foul smell from her. King Harald ordered a funeral pyre to be quickly arranged. Before she was burnt her body turned blue, and worms, adders, frogs and toads and *'all manner of foul reptiles'* were seen to crawl out of her. The magic of the Finn man and his daughter was then exposed to King Harald, and he drove away the sons that they had had together. He was later persuaded to accept these sons back, as a friend pointed out that they would have had a better mother if Harald had given them one.

King Harald Fair-hair's new kingdom was subject to attack from Viking raiders who lived in the islands to the west of Norway. Shetland, Orkney and the Hebrides were used as bases from which to raid Norway, and it was said that many of these Vikings were the former chieftains who had been driven out by Harald. The king decided that action must be taken, and he ordered a great battle fleet to sail west to purge the islands of Vikings. This happened sometime around the year 874, when King Harald finally subdued all of Norway. With him on this great expedition were Earl Rognvald of More and his son Ivar. First they sailed to Shetland, as it is told in *Heimskringla 'and there slew all the Vikings who had not fled hence'*. Then they sailed south to Orkney, *'and cleansed them all of Vikings'*. Next the Hebrides and Scotland were attacked. King Harald is said to have sailed as far south as the Isle of Man, where he found the island deserted, as the population had fled to Scotland with everything that they could carry.

Earl Rognvald of More's son Ivar was killed in one of the battles. *Landnamabok* (The Book of Settlements) says his death occurred in the Hebrides. King Harald gave Earl Rognvald the islands of Orkney and Shetland in compensation for the loss of his son. *Vatnsdœla Saga* (The Saga of the People of Vatnsdal) records the event:

> He rewarded Rognvald with an earldom and said, "You have shown great courage in your support for me; you have also lost your son for my sake, and he cannot be restored to you, but I can reward you with honours – firstly by making you an earl, and also by giving you those islands which lie to the west, and are called the Orkney Islands. You shall have those islands as compensation for your son; and you will receive many another honour from me."

Earl Rognvald held considerable estates in Norway, and maybe he felt that these islands would prove more of a curse than a blessing, as he had to defend them from Viking raiders. He gave the islands to his brother Sigurd, and King Harald gave Sigurd the title of earl.

How much of this story is true, and how much is myth? There are no contemporary accounts of this great expedition from either Britain or Ireland that would support the claim. Events like these were recorded, albeit briefly, in church records. This story could have been confused with King Magnus Barelegs' expedition in 1098, which we will read about later.[2] These events were recorded centuries after they were supposed to have happened, and different sagas give very different versions of events. Take the case of Ketil Flat-nose.

In *Eyrbyggja Saga* (The Saga of the People of Eyri) Ketil Flat-nose was said to be a powerful chieftain in Norway at the time of King Harald Fair-hair. Raids on Norway from Shetland, Orkney and the Hebrides became so frequent that the farmers pleaded for help from the king. He raised an army and called Ketil Flat-nose to lead it. Ketil tried his best to get out of the command, but, on seeing that the king would have his way, he reluctantly agreed. He left Norway with the army, taking his wife and the children who still lived at home with him. He fought several battles in the west and always had the victory. On reaching the Hebrides he established himself as ruler and formed alliances with the most powerful leaders there. He sent the army back to Norway, where they told King Harald that Ketil had taken control of the Hebrides, but that it was not clear whether he had done it in the king's name or not. King Harald was furious and seized Ketil's estate in Norway.

Ketil's son Bjorn drove away King Harald's agents from his father's estate and claimed it as his own. King Harald had him declared an outlaw, and he had to flee for his life. He was sheltered by a chieftain called Thorolf who lived on the island of Mostor off southern Hordaland. Thorolf took his name from the god Thor, whom he worshipped in a temple he had built in the god's honour, but his actual name was Hrolf. He was also nicknamed Moster-beard, due to his huge whiskers and the island he came from. When King Harald found out that Thorolf Moster-beard had sheltered Bjorn he ordered that Thorolf should come and submit to him or become an outlaw. Thorolf sacrificed to Thor and asked for advice. The oracle told him to go to Iceland, and he followed this advice. As he neared land he threw the high-seat pillars from Thor's temple over the side of the ship to let the god guide him. They travelled at great speed around Snaefellsnes on the west coast, coming to rest at a place that he called Thorsnes (Thor's headland) in Breidafjord (Broad Fjord). Here Thorolf built his temple and settled.

---

[2] Thomson, William P.L. *A New History of Orkney.* Mercat Press, Edinburgh, 2001. 25–39.

In *Laxdæla Saga* (The Saga of the People of Laxardal) we have a very different story about Ketil Flat-nose. He was a powerful chieftain who was getting on in years when King Harald started his campaign to claim all of Norway. He called a meeting to ask his kinsmen how they felt about surrendering their lands to King Harald. Ketil's son Bjorn spoke out strongly against it; his opinion was that they should leave rather than let that happen. They applauded his words, saying that he had spoken boldly, and it was decided that they would leave Norway rather than be in King Harald's power. Bjorn, his brother Helgi, their sister Thorunn and her husband Helgi the Lean decided to go to Iceland and to start a new life there. Ketil Flat-nose and the others decided to go to Scotland to live. In this version it was Bjorn's high-seat pillars that were washed up in Breidafjord in western Iceland, and not Thorolf Moster-beard's.

Here we have two very different versions of events. One in which Ketil leads the army, then takes control for himself, the other where he is one of the chieftains driven out of Norway by King Harald. There is a third version in *Landnamabok* where King Harald leads an army west, but after his return to Norway, the Hebrides were invaded by *'Vikings, Scots and Irishmen.'* Ketil was sent to bring the Hebrides back under King Harald's control, but after he was victorious he claimed the islands as his own and sent no tribute east to the king. Harald had his estate confiscated and his son Bjorn driven out of it.

The story of Ketil Flat-nose is a good example of how sagas can contradict one another. If we return to the *Orkneyinga Saga* we don't find Ketil Flat-nose mentioned, but we do find his daughter, Aud the Deep-minded. She is one of the great matriarchs of saga literature, and the ancestor of many of the leading families in Orkney, Faeroes and Iceland. She went to the

Aerial view of Sanday – Keith Allardyce

Hebrides with her father and married Olaf the White, described in *Eyrbyggia Saga* as *'the greatest warlord in the Western Isles.'* Their son was Thorstein the Red, who made an alliance with the newly-appointed earl of Orkney, Sigurd the Powerful (the brother of Earl Rognvald of More). The *Orkneyinga Saga* tells how these two warriors raided in Scotland until they had captured all of Caithness and a large part of Argyll, Moray and Ross. Earl Sigurd had a stronghold built near present-day Inverness. The fact that Ketil Flat-nose had a grown-up grandson at the time of King Harald's expedition west suggests that he belonged to an earlier generation than King Harald Fair-hair.

The *Orkneyinga Saga* says that a Scottish earl called Mælbrigte Tusk had arranged talks with Sigurd, and it was agreed that they should meet with 40 mounted warriors each. This meeting was to take place sometime between the years 891–894. Earl Sigurd didn't trust the Scots, and he mounted two men to each horse. When Mælbrigte Tusk saw two pairs of legs hanging by the side of every horse he knew that he had been tricked, and he urged his men to each kill at least one of the Norsemen before they died. Sigurd ordered half of the troop to dismount and to make their way behind the Scots. Facing armed warriors on two fronts it wasn't long before the Scots were cut down. Earl Sigurd ordered the heads of the slain Scots to be cut off and fastened to his men's saddlebows, as a show of their victory. Earl Sigurd cut off Earl Mælbrigte Tusk's head himself and fastened it to his own saddle. Mælbrigte had got the name 'Tusk' because he had a large tooth that protruded from his mouth. As Earl Sigurd spurred his horse onwards the head swung against his calf and the protruding tooth caused a scratch. Blood poisoning set into the wound and this led to the death of Earl Sigurd the Powerful. He was buried in a great mound by the side of the River Oykel in Sutherland.

Aikerness, Evie – Raymond Parks

It is interesting to note that the motif of cutting off the heads of enemies and boasting of their deaths is a Celtic custom. It has been argued that a Celtic folktale of how the severed head takes its revenge on the killer was the original inspiration behind this story in the *Orkneyinga Saga*. We should bear in mind that there was contact between the Scandinavian and Celtic worlds, and that tales would have passed between them.[3]

According to the *Laxdæla Saga,* Earl Sigurd's partner, Thorstein the Red, was killed by the Scots in Caithness. His mother, Aud the Deep-minded (called Unn in *Laxdæla Saga*), was staying in Caithness at the time. Knowing the danger that she was now in, Aud had a longship built secretly in a forest. When it was ready she sailed with a group of people to Orkney, where she arranged the marriage of her granddaughter Groa, Thorstein the Red's daughter. *Heimskringla* says that Groa was not married in Orkney, but that her husband was Dungad (Duncan) the earl of Duncansbay in Caithness. Groa had a daughter called Grelod who would marry the Orkney earl, Thorfinn Skull-splitter. Aud then sailed to the Faeroes, where she married Olof, another daughter of Thorstein the Red, to one of the most prominent families in the islands. According to the *Færeyinga Saga* (the Saga of the Faeroe Islanders) it was from this marriage of Olof that the family known as the Gate-beards who lived on the island of Eastrey were descended. Other daughters of Thorstein the Red were married into prominent families in Iceland. By the shrewd selection of husbands for her granddaughters, Aud had ensured that her family was connected with some of the most powerful dynasties in the northern world.

Earl Sigurd the Powerful was succeeded as earl of Orkney by his son Guthorm, who ruled the islands for a year before dying childless. When Earl Rognvald of More heard that his brother and nephew had died he sent one of his illegitimate sons, Hallad, to Orkney. King Harald Fair-hair granted him the title of earl, but Hallad soon found that he simply could not control the situation. Vikings continued to raid the islands, causing the farmers to complain to Earl Hallad that they needed protection. Earl Hallad thought that this was beyond his power, and he gave up the earldom and returned to Norway in shame. The islands then fell into the hands of two Danish Vikings called Thorir Tree-beard and Kalf Scurvy.

---

[3] Almqvist, Bo. 'Scandinavian and Celtic Contacts in the Earldom of Orkney', *Viking Ale; Studies on Folklore Contacts between Northern and the Western Worlds.* Boethius Press, Wales, 1991. 1–29.

VIKING GRAVES

The Viking movement began at the end of the eighth century, when the Scandinavian lands were still pagan. Pagan Vikings tended to bury their dead fully clothed, wearing jewellery and accompanied with a range of grave-goods including weapons and household items, and even animals and boats.

Grave-goods may have been items that the person would need in their 'next' life, or it could have been a sign of the family's high status to give their dead a rich burial, or they could have been 'cult' objects showing the dead person's relationship with the gods. The goods in the grave may have belonged to the dead person in life, or they could have come from other members of the family. The goods in the grave at Scar in Sanday were almost all old and worn when they were buried, except for one sandstone spindle-whorl that seems to have been completely new.

Pagan Viking graves have been found in Orkney in Westray, Sanday, Rousay and the Mainland.

Graves were found in the Links to the north of Pierowall in Westray as gales eroded the sandy soil. Some were recorded by James Wallace in the seventeenth century, others by George Low in the eighteenth century and George Petrie in the nineteenth century. The cemetery must have contained at least 17 graves and very probably more, making it one of the most extensive Viking cemeteries found in Scotland. It was said to have included burials with horses and dogs, and some boat burials, as well as the usual range of jewellery, weaponry and household goods.[1]

A cemetery was found at Westness in Rousay in 1963, when a richly-furnished woman's grave was disturbed by Ronald Stevenson of Westness, who was burying a cow. The woman had been buried with a new-born baby, so she may have died in childbirth. She wore a pair of oval brooches and a necklace of glass beads, and had Anglo-Saxon strap ends on her belt and a magnificent silver-gilt brooch which may have been made in Ireland or in Pictland. She also had a comb and a bronze basin, and working tools including a sickle and weaving gear. Subsequent seasons of excavation revealed a cemetery of the Pictish and early Viking period. The earlier graves had no grave goods, and may have been Christian, but some of the Viking-period graves did not have grave goods either, so perhaps the real explanation is more complicated. The later burials seem to have respected the earlier ones and were not cut into them, perhaps suggesting continuity in the community.

There were two boat burials at Westness, each containing a man. One of the men had the remains of four arrows in his body and the shield boss of the other man had been badly slashed, probably in a fight. Though the men seem to have been fighters, they were also buried with farming and fishing gear. Other men and women were buried in oval graves that were lined with stones to represent boats. Apart from the jewellery they wore, their typical grave goods included weapons and farming tools for men, and spinning and weaving equipment for women. Sickles were found in the graves of men and women, showing the importance of the harvest.[2]

The Viking woman's grave found at the Broch of Gurness in the 1930s may have been part of a larger cemetery, for there are indications of more Viking graves on the site.[3] The woman was buried in a stone-lined cist, with a knife and a sickle. She wore oval brooches made of copper-alloy and she had an iron necklet. The necklet is now very badly corroded, but it seems to have had an amulet in the shape of a Thor's hammer. Necklets like these are not known in Scotland but they are found in Sweden.[4]

Viking period graves and buildings have also been found around the north side of Birsay Bay, on the Point of Buckquoy. One man's grave contained a fine Irish ringed pin and half of an

Anglo-Saxon silver penny of the 940s.[5] In a nearby grave the body may have been disturbed or even desecrated, for one of the arm-bones had been turned the wrong way round, and the fine Viking comb lay in the skeleton's mouth.[6]

The boat burial at Scar in Sanday was found and excavated in 1991. It is unusual in that the boat contained the remains of three people. A child of about ten and a woman in her eighties had been laid in the middle of the boat, and a man in his thirties lay crouched at the end. The grave was half eroded by the sea and it had been badly disturbed by otters, but enough remained to show that it was a well-equipped grave, including merchants' weights and gaming pieces. The man had his weapons and the woman her sickle, sewing and weaving equipment and the magnificent Scar linen-smoothing plaque made of whale bone. Plaques like this are mostly found in northern Norway, in richly-furnished graves of women.[7] The woman's fine brooch is also of a north Norwegian type,[8] but it was old and worn when it was buried. She may originally have had other jewellery, but that part of the grave was particularly badly disturbed by the otters. The Scar grave dates from the late ninth or early tenth century, contemporary with the earlier years of the saga.[9]

Anne Brundle

---

[1] Arne Thorsteinsson 1968. Graham-Campbell and Batey 1998, 129 – 134.

[2] Kaland 1993, 314

[3] Hedges J W, 1987, 73

[4] Graham-Campbell and Batey 1998, 128

[5] Ritchie 1977, 190-1

[6] Morris 1989, 200 and Illus 85-6

[7] Owen and Dalland, 1999, 80

[8] ibid, 68

[9] ibid, 188

Westness-woman's grave goods assemblage, excavated 1963 – National Museums of Scotand

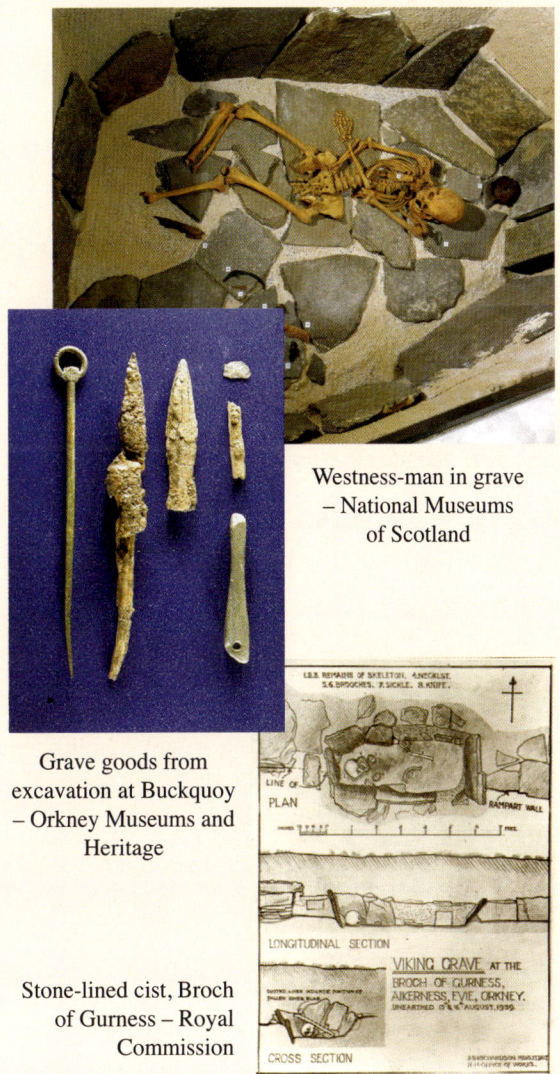

Westness-man in grave – National Museums of Scotland

Grave goods from excavation at Buckquoy – Orkney Museums and Heritage

Stone-lined cist, Broch of Gurness – Royal Commission

SCAR BOAT BURIAL

Scar Plaque

Needle case

Weaving batten

Iron shears and steatite spindle whorl

Brooch

Sword

Sword hilt

WOMAN

MAN

The Scar Boat Burial excavation in situ – Richard Welsby

Gaming pieces

Arrows

Scar boat burial

The Viking boat burial at Scar in Sanday was found in the autumn of 1991, eroding out of the low-lying coastline. It was at severe risk of being washed away by seasonal gales so it was excavated that winter, from October to December, by a team of archaeologists from AOC Scotland led by Magnar Dalland.

The excavation showed the remains of a boat grave that lay parallel to the coastline, but one side had been completely washed away. Unusually, the grave contained the remains of three people. The bodies of an elderly woman and of a child of about ten had been laid in the centre of the boat, and the body of a man in his thirties was crouched in the end of the grave space.

The burials were richly furnished with grave goods. The man had been buried with a sword and a bundle of arrows that were probably in a quiver. Fragmentary remains found with him may have been part of a shield. He held a comb between his hands and nearby there was a bundle of gaming-pieces and some merchant's weights.

The burials of the woman and the child had been badly disturbed by otters that had nested in the grave-space. The woman would probably have been buried wearing jewellery but the only piece that was found was an equal-armed brooch. It was made of copper alloy that had been gilded on the front, and would have had fourteen silver bosses where only nails remain. It seems most likely that she was buried wearing it, but it was found face-down at her right side. She had a comb similar to the man's but less well-preserved. There was a sickle for cutting grain and also at her right side were her sewing and weaving gear, including iron shears, stone spindle whorls, a needlecase and a weaving batten. The magnificent whale-bone smoothing plaque had been propped up at her feet but had fallen forward, which may have helped preserve it.

The bodies had been laid in a boat that had been buried in the sand and packed round with stones. All the wood of the boat had rotted away but the iron rivets remained and showed that the boat had been built of overlapping oak planks, perhaps with a washrail of pine. The pattern of the rivets showed that the boat had been repaired in the past.

The whale-bone plaque and the equal-armed brooch both suggest cultural links with northern Norway. The stylistic attributes of the artefacts group them in the ninth century, the early part of the Viking Age, but the carbon-dating evidence suggests that they were buried much later, perhaps in the middle of the tenth century.

Anne Brundle

Reference: Owen, O and Dalland, M, 1999, *Scar - A Viking Boat Burial on Sanday, Orkney*, Tuckwell Press in Association with Historic Scotland, East Linton.

TURF EINAR AND THE SONS OF KING HARALD

The events in this chapter take place c.891–c.991. After the death of Earl Sigurd and his son, Earl Rognvald of More sent his own illegitimate son Turf Einar to Orkney as earl. This was a dangerous time, as the numerous sons of King Harald Fair-hair fought for the control of their father's kingdom. Earl Rognvald of More was murdered by two of King Harald's sons, but his death was avenged by Turf Einar, who killed one of them in North Ronaldsay. Another of King Harald's sons, Erik Blood-axe, was killed along with two of Turf Einar's sons while raiding in England. Erik's daughter was married to one of the Orkney earls, but she caused murder and civil war that nearly wiped out the descendants of Turf Einar.

Earl Rognvald of More had several sons. By his wife Ragnhild (called by the shortened name Hild in *Heimskringla*) he had three sons – Ivar (who was killed on the expedition west), Hrolf and Thorir the Silent (called Tore in *Heimskringla*). He also had three illegitimate sons – Hallad, Hrollaug and Einar. The *Orkneyinga Saga* says that Einar was the youngest of these sons, while both *Heimskringla* and *Landnamabok* say that he was the middle child. *Heimskringla* says that these three illegitimate sons were fully grown when the three sons by Rognvald's marriage to Ragnhild were still children.

Peat cutting, Sandwick – Keith Allardyce

When Hallad gave up the earldom of Orkney, Earl Rognvald was furious. He called his sons to him to decide who should go to the islands as the earl of Orkney in Hallad's place. Hrolf was away on a Viking raid at the time. Thorir said that it should be up to their father to choose who should go. Earl Rognvald said that Thorir should stay in Norway and inherit the earldom of More after Rognvald's death. Hrollaug asked if he should go to Orkney, but Rognvald said that his fate was to go to Iceland where he would become a great man. The last to ask was Einar, Earl Rognvald's least favourite son. The *Orkneyinga Saga* describes him as:

> ...a tall man, and ugly, one-eyed, yet of all men the most keen-sighted.

He made his father an offer he couldn't refuse: to go away from Norway so that Rognvald would never have to see him again. Earl Rognvald liked that suggestion, and agreed to it at once, saying that Einar was unlikely to succeed in Norway as his mother and all her family were slave-born. Earl Rognvald gave Einar a fully equipped ship of twenty benches, and King Harald Fair-hair gave him the title of earl of Orkney. Einar sailed to Shetland in the harvest time, then south to Orkney. *Heimskringla* says that Einar met the Danish Vikings, Thorir Tree-beard and Kalf Scurvy, in two ships. He attacked and won the victory, killing both of the Viking leaders. Einar was now secure in Orkney.

Hoxa, South Ronaldsay – John Brundle

The story of Earl Rognvald and his sons is interesting, as Rognvald is credited with predicting their future fate. What happened to them was well known to the saga writers, so this was probably inserted later. This version appears in the *Orkneyinga Saga* and *Landnamabok*, but not in *Heimskringla* where Einar offers to go away, much to the delight of his father. The version in *Landnamabok* has Hrolf there with his brothers, but his offer to go to Orkney as the earl is rejected by his father who thinks that he is too hot tempered and violent to be a ruler. As this man went on to conquer the part of France which became known as Normandy (named after the 'north men' who ruled it), becoming its first duke and the ancestor of William the Conqueror, then maybe Earl Rognvald was not so good at predictions after all.

Einar gained himself a nickname, being called Turf Einar. This was said to be because he was the first person to cut peats (called 'torf' in Old Norse) for fuel, as there were no trees in Orkney. It is said that he cut peat at Tarbat Ness in Easter Ross, but there is no shortage of peat in Orkney. Peat has been cut and dried as fuel since prehistoric times, so it certainly was not Einar who introduced the practice. In both the *Orkneyinga Saga* and *Heimskringla* we find a verse composed by Einar after the defeat of the Danish Vikings when he first arrived in Orkney:

> He gave Tree-beard to the trolls;
> Turf-Einar slew Scurvy.

This suggests that he was already called Turf Einar before he came to Orkney. Why he was called that we will never know. Could it be that as the illegitimate son of a slave woman he was held in such low esteem by his father that he was given menial tasks to perform around the house? Maybe he was in charge of cutting peats for the family fire, although in a heavily wooded area this is unlikely.

King Harald Fair-hair's numerous sons were proving to be a bit of a handful. Halfdan High-legs and Gudrod Gleam were two of the sons that King Harald had with the Finn woman Snæfrid. They were jealous of the earls that their father had put in charge of the regions of Norway, thinking that they themselves should be given the land to rule. They attacked the earls, killing them or driving them away and claiming the land as their own. *Heimskringla* gives more information than the *Orkneyinga Saga* about the fate of Earl Rognvald of More. One spring Halfdan and Gudrod gathered together a great band of warriors and attacked the earl in More. They surrounded the house and burnt it, killing Earl Rognvald and sixty of his men. Gudrod then claimed all of Earl Rognvald's land and settled himself there, while Halfdan took three longships and sailed west to Orkney. King Harald Fair-hair was so furious about the killing of his friend Earl Rognvald that he set off with an army against Gudrod. Seeing no way of escaping his father's wrath, Gudrod had to plead for his life. He was sent east out of his father's way. King Harald gave the title of earl to Rognvald's son Thorir the Silent, and the king also gave his daughter Alof in marriage to Thorir.

The *Orkneyinga Saga* says that Halfdan and his warriors drove Earl Turf Einar out of Orkney, forcing him to hide in Caithness. Halfdan then ruled Orkney, and the people there took him as their leader. Turf Einar returned that harvest time and fought Halfdan in a short sea battle off North Ronaldsay. Halfdan was defeated and fled under the cover of darkness. Turf Einar composed poems shaming his brothers for not avenging their father, especially Thorir, the new earl of More, who sat silently drinking at home as the battle raged.

The following morning Turf Einar saw movement on North Ronaldsay; something was rising up then falling back to earth. He ordered his men to search the island where they found Halfdan. Einar killed him in the most horrific way, by carving a blood-eagle on his back. His ribs were cut away on both sides of the spine, and then his lungs were drawn out and spread out like the wings of an eagle. Turf Einar composed verses over the dead prince, taunting King Harald Fairhair over the killing of his son. Here it is thought that the saga writer was trying to compare Earl Turf Einar with the god Odin. Odin had sacrificed an eye in order to gain wisdom, while Einar was one-eyed, but was still keen-sighted. Odin was also the god of poetry. Odin was no longer worshipped when this was written, but he was still known to medieval audiences. In the mythological *Saga of the Volsungs* we find Odin playing an important role. This popular saga tells of the family of King Volsung, the ancestor of the popular hero Sigurd the Dragon-slayer. In the saga, Odin appears at crucial moments to give victory or bring death. While Odin is named to start with, later in the *Saga of the Volsungs* it just refers to him as a one-eyed man, but the audience would have known who it was meant to be. To underline the comparison in the *Orkneyinga Saga*, Einar sacrifices Halfdan to Odin in gratitude for his victory. It is from

North Ronaldsay – Keith Allardyce

this man, the lowly born Turf Einar, that the earls of Orkney are descended, and the saga writer wanted to leave no doubts about the suitability of Einar as a powerful and worthy ancestor.[4]

King Harald led another expedition west to Orkney to avenge his son's death. Earl Turf Einar fled to Caithness, but a peace settlement was arranged, and compensation agreed. King Harald issued a fine of 60 gold marks on the islands. Turf Einar offered to pay the whole fine himself if the bonders (landowners) would give up their odal rights to him. This meant that people held their land from the earl and had to pay him taxes.

Earl Turf Einar had three sons, Arnkel, Erlend and Thorfinn Skull-splitter. *Landnamabok* says that he had a daughter in his youth called Thordis. She was raised by her grandfather, Earl Rognvald of More, who married her to Thorgeir the Clumsy. They had a son called Einar who travelled to Orkney to see his 'kinsmen,' probably his uncles, but they refused to accept him. He bought a share in a ship and sailed to Iceland where he settled. Turf Einar ruled Orkney for many years and died in his bed.

Of all of King Harald Fair-hair's sons, Erik Blood-axe was his favourite. *Heimskringla* records how the king had given him five longships to go raiding, when Erik was only twelve years old. While he was raiding in Finmark, Erik's men found a woman in a turf hut who was exceptionally beautiful. She said that her name was Gunnhild, and that she had been sent there to learn witchcraft from two Finn men. They were the most powerful sorcerers and could out-ski and out-shoot anyone; they could even kill a man just by staring at him. Gunnhild hid Erik's men and tricked the Finns into falling asleep on either side of her. She tied sealskin bags over their heads as they slept, then Erik's men killed them and took Gunnhild to Erik who later married her. This tale resembles the marriage of King Harald Fair-hair and Snæfrid, portraying Gunnhild as an evil and dangerous woman.

Erik had been given the kingdom of Norway to rule when his father was too old and frail, but he was a violent and overbearing man and unpopular. After the death of King Harald Fair-hair in the year 934, Erik ruled for two years before being driven out by his half-brother, Hakon the Good, who had been fostered by the English King Athelstan. Erik Blood-axe fled overseas and raided in Scotland and England before accepting the kingdom of Northumbria from King Athelstan. He had offered the kingdom to Erik because he had been a good friend of King Harald Fair-hair's, and he hoped to bring about a truce between his foster-son Hakon and Erik. After King Athelstan's death the kingdom of England was ruled by his brother Edmund. He had no love for the Norsemen, and resented Erik Blood-axe having Northumbria. One spring Erik travelled to Orkney and collected the earls Arnkel and Erlend. They set off raiding with a great force in Ireland, Wales and England. They plundered and raided through England with a great army of warriors, as Erik had heard that King Edmund planned to drive him from Northumbria. A regional ruler called Olaf gathered together a huge army to attack King Erik's force. They met in a bloody battle where the greater numbers of English warriors proved decisive. King Erik Blood-axe was killed, along with five other kings and the Orkney earls Arnkel and Erlend.

---

[4] Thomson, William P.L. *The New History of Orkney.* Mercat Press, Edinburgh, 2001. 35–39.

When Queen Gunnhild heard that her husband had been killed while raiding in England she knew that she and her sons were no longer safe in Northumbria. They sailed north to Orkney, where Thorfinn Skull-splitter was now the sole earl. The *Orkneyinga Saga* says:

> Gunnhild's sons now subdued the Isles. They spent the winters in them, but in summer went a-harrying.

This implies that Earl Thorfinn Skull-splitter had handed power over to them while they were in Orkney. News eventually reached Gunnhild that war had broken out between King Hakon the Good of Norway and King Harald of Denmark. Seeing an opportunity of gaining power, Gunnhild and her sons left Orkney to side with the Danish king. Thorfinn Skull-splitter was now back in charge of his earldom. He was a mighty chieftain and ruled for many years before dying in his bed in 976. He was buried at Hoxa in South Ronaldsay.

Heimskringla records the fate of Gunnhild and the sons of Erik Blood-axe. Although they all met violent deaths, some at least did become kings in Norway. Gunnhild's greed was such that she taunted them until they made war on powerful enemies, which led to defeat and exile in Orkney once more before their deaths. Before Gunnhild left Orkney the first time, around the year 956, she sowed the seeds of civil war in the islands by marrying her daughter Ragnhild to Earl Thorfinn Skull-splitter's son Arnfinn. He was the oldest of Earl Thorfinn's sons, the other four being Havard Harvest-happy, Hlodver, Ljot and Skuli. The *Orkneyinga Saga* claims that Ragnhild was every bit as ambitious, greedy and treacherous as her mother. It is worth remembering, though, that the sagas, like many histories, were written by the winning side, and that personal grudges and feuds can colour the way in which the story is told.

Ragnhild now embarked on a career as a professional widow. Firstly she arranged the murder of her husband Arnfinn at Murkle in Caithness. She then offered herself in marriage to his younger brother, Havard Harvest-happy. He became a popular earl who ruled during a period of good harvests, hence his nickname. Ragnhild soon got fed up with him too, and had secret meetings with his nephew, Einar Butter-bread, who was the son of Havard's sister. She said that he was a great chief and should kill his uncle Havard and claim the earldom for himself. She also offered herself in marriage to him if he took the earldom. Spurred on by Ragnhild, Einar met his uncle Havard in battle somewhere in Stenness. It was a short and bloody affair, which ended in the death of Havard Harvest-happy. Einar Butter-bread now claimed the earldom, and Ragnhild, as his prize. She immediately refused, denying that she had any part in her husband's killing. She went to another nephew of her late husband, his sister's son Einar Hard-chaps, to avenge the killing of his uncle. She again hinted at marriage to the killer, so Einar Hard-chaps killed his cousin Einar Butter-bread. He was ill-rewarded for avenging the killing of Havard Harvest-happy; Ragnhild now married another former brother-in-law, Ljot. Einar Hard-chaps tried to raise an army to fight Ljot, but the earl had him captured and put to death.

Sometime around the year 978, Ljot's brother Skuli went to see the King of Scotland, from whom he received the earldom of Caithness. He gathered an army together and sailed to Orkney where he argued with his brother over the earldom. Ljot in turn raised an army and marched against Skuli. They fought a hard battle, but with superior forces Ljot won the day and Skuli fled south to Caithness, and then to the king of Scots. The king and Earl Macbeth[5] gave him a large army with which to fight Ljot. The two brothers met at the Dales in Caithness where they fought a great battle. The Scots fought fiercely, but Ljot held his ground. Urging his men on, Ljot led a fierce attack against the Scots, breaking their line and causing them to flee. Skuli tried to make one last stand, but was killed. Ljot now claimed Caithness as his own, an action that angered the king of Scots. While Ljot's forces were still in a weakened state they were attacked at Skitten Mire[6] in Caithness by the Scottish Earl Macbeth who had gathered a great army. Ljot's battered band of warriors was in no fit state to fight a battle, but he had no choice. Earl Ljot led such a fierce attack against the Scots that many were killed and wounded, and the rest fled for their lives. Ljot had won the day against great odds, but he had received a wound that led to his death. He was much lamented in Orkney. His brother Hlodver succeeded him as earl of Orkney, and was considered a mighty chief. He was married to Eithne, the daughter of King Kjarval of Ireland, and they had a son called Sigurd the Stout who inherited the earldom after his father's death.

[5] An unknown Scottish chieftain, possibly from Moray.

[6] Now called the Moss of Killimster near Wick.

Looking south from the Mainland of Orkney to Hoy – Raymond Parks

BIRSAY: THE BROUGH AND THE

The Brough of Birsay is an iconic site that has attracted the attention of many archaeologists from Sir Henry Dryden in the late nineteenth century through to contemporaries John Hunter and Chris Morris in the later twentieth century. Their successive works, often examining the works of their predecessors, have given us huge amounts of information about the site.

The words "broch" and "Brough" both have their derivations from the Old Norse word *borg* meaning a fortified place. Spelling conventions have resolved "Brough" as meaning a peninsula or island – which is the meaning of the word in this case. "Broch" is used when making reference to the many Iron Age 'tower houses'. The word Birsay - "*Byrgisherad*" in the *Orkneyinga Saga*, includes the "borg" element, maybe a reference to naming the parish from the Brough.

All the excavators on the Brough of Birsay were constrained by the need to leave good structural remains in place to be conserved for display. This often required them to leave earlier remains incompletely examined. Nonetheless, they have demonstrated a long and complex story of people living on the island for 500 years and more.

Nearby, important work related to the Pictish/Viking interface (not gone into here) was undertaken on sites between the road to the Brough and the sea by Anna Ritchie during the 1970s; most of these sites are now invisible, or eroded away. On the Brough, several Pictish buildings have also been examined, though none are now displayed. Apart from the reproduction of the superb symbol stone in the churchyard, a small well on the east side of the church is now all that can be seen from the Pictish period on the site itself. There is, however, an unusual richness in the artefacts which came from the Pictish levels, including many bronze objects; evidence, in the form of moulds, for the making of jewellery; and evidence for glass working. Similar richness was not demonstrated in the Brough road sites. It is clear that the Brough itself was an important centre in the seventh and eighth centuries.

The arrival of the Vikings in the ninth century marked the beginning of the great change to Orkney becoming Norse and officially part of the Norwegian kingdom, probably sometime towards the end of the ninth century. This change is marked most strongly in the

Brough of Birsay – Richard Welsby

VILLAGE

archaeological record by the change from essentially round or curvy house styles of the Pictish and earlier periods to that of the near rectangular long-house.

The Brough of Birsay is one of the few places where the foundations of Viking style houses can still be seen. The layout here, as elsewhere, is almost invariably to align the houses up and down the hill, across the contours. They lie on the hillside above and to the SW of the chapel. The walls of these houses were constructed with stone inner faces and a jacket of turf. These walls would probably never have been very high. The roofs were supported by a double row of posts on the interior, and would have extended over the outer turf walls. Inside, a long hearth centrally placed would have burnt mostly peat. Each side of the fire were benches or platforms for sitting and sleeping. In some houses the cattle would be kept in the lower end, whilst the people lived in the upper.

The apparently simple plan of these houses, as they are now presented, is a bit misleading. For instance, the two most south-westerly houses are of the ninth century. They probably developed as a pair, with a narrow passageway in between them. The outermost of the two was a house and byre, with the readily understandable arrangement of living area at the top, with cattle housed below. The second of the pair was extended, perhaps in the tenth or eleventh century, by an additional room at the top end. Inside, some areas were demarcated as separate by upright flagstones. Likewise, the other early buildings on the site have quite complex histories.

Because earlier excavations of the interiors of some of the inland buildings had destroyed some of the more subtle evidence, the excavations of some of the eroding, coast-edge buildings can fill gaps, unpicking the changes to the design of the houses, and demonstrating subdivision and alteration of structures through time. Here it was also demonstrated, for instance, that one building had been used as a smithy. In another of the buildings examined by Morris on the coastal fringe (outside the Guardianship area) many rivets were found. These have been interpreted as having come from re-used ship timbers having been incorporated into the building. This was a common practice until recently in Orkney, where the lack of large trees led to every scrap of decent wood being used and re-used. Other speculative interpretations, such as this being a carpenter's workshop, would also be entirely possible.

During the Viking period, only outsiders made any written history. Viking operations in Orkney are effectively prehistoric, until we come to the Norse period, when we get the Sagas. Of the many places in Orkney which were written about in the *Orkneyinga Saga*, Birsay is amongst the most important. The first time it is mentioned is in the time of Thorfinn in the eleventh century. This concerns his establishment of a minster at Birsay, and the construction of a magnificent church dedicated to Christ. The grandeur of this would have been a reflection of the consolidation and extension of his power throughout Orkney and beyond – as the saga says, by the time of his death he had "won for himself nine Scottish earldoms along with the whole of the Hebrides, and a considerable part of Ireland."

It is worth remembering that the *Orkneyinga Saga* was compiled in Iceland a couple of hundred years or more after the main events it described. Thus it is very useful to have occasional external confirmations of people and places as being real happenings. The reference to the establishment of Thorfinn's Birsay as the centre of the Orkney church in the *Orkneyinga Saga* is lent much credibility by his near contemporary Adam of Bremen, who wrote in his *History of the Archbishops of Hamburg-*

Bremen of the establishment of the bishop in Birsay "consecrating Throlf bishop for the city of Birsay, and he was to have the cure of all" [of the Orkney Islands].

The remains of the church on the Brough represent what is left of a small but sophisticated building. It consists of a rectangular nave with side altars, a chancel and an apse, which once would have been barrel-vaulted like St Nicholas church in Papa Stronsay, or the remaining part of the round church in Orphir. The main altar was moved from the chancel into the nave at some point during its use. It probably had a square tower on its west end. Its Romanesque style dates it to the twelfth century, possibly the earlier part.

To the north of the church is a series of buildings aligned with, and at right angles to, the church. Here, walls of formally arranged and spacious buildings enclose three sides of a rectangular open space, of which the nave forms the fourth side. These buildings have been said to represent the remains of a monastery with cloister. Equally, the layout of the enclosure is said to be very similar to that of the bishop's palace established at Gardar in Greenland in the earlier twelfth century, where large halls and grain stores were arranged next to the church. Whichever interpretation is correct, it would certainly appear that the church and buildings were laid out as a unified whole.

The many walls and buildings conserved below the Church on the Brough represent remains from the ninth to twelfth centuries. Because they are of a variety of periods, they are not that easy to understand on the ground. The added complexity is that no-longer was a single open hall a desirable building. From the eleventh century onwards, the main long-hearthed hall was often sub-divided, and many small, additional rooms were added. This increased the length of the buildings substantially through time. Also, many rooms were often added to the side of the buildings, or outbuildings were made, often with specialist uses. Thus from simple beginnings, the Norse farm can develop into a rather straggly complex.

One notable building on the Brough is the "bath house" or sauna building. This element in particular has been used to suggest that the farm settlement represented by the buildings may be of a particularly high status. Another noteworthy feature, (now somewhat shortened by coastal erosion) is the grand, paved, entrance-way to the Brough. It has been suggested that this may have been used as a means of drawing boats up, and, if the width of the entrance is related to the size of boat, this might mean that we are dealing here with further evidence for a high status settlement. Similarities can be seen between this complex of buildings and those which grew up at Jarlshof, Shetland, or Brattahlid, Greenland, founded by Eric the Red at the end of the tenth century. These comparisons have led some to argue that some of these remains, therefore, represent those of Thorfinn's hall and church.

One of the main debates about the Brough of Birsay is related to whether or not Thorfinn's hall and church were built on the island, or within the area which is on the east side of the Bay, and is now a village.

There are two contenders for the position of Thorfinn's Christchurch – that traditionally dedicated to St Peter on the island or under the present church of St Magnus in the village. Archaeologically or historically, there is as yet no definitive answer as to which is truly Thorfinn's minster. The church visible on the Brough appears to have been founded in the twelfth century, (too late to be Thorfinn's minster) but it overlies an earlier building, which might also be a church.

The church in the village also has earlier (possibly twelfth century) foundations beneath it. It is to be noted that many of the people of Birsay, up to today, have referred to the church in the village by the name of Christkirk. George Low, writing in the eighteenth century, speaks of a large cross-shaped church having once stood there, and of the likelihood that the village of Birsay and its palace sites are where Thorfinn's church and place of residence once stood.

The *Orkneyinga Saga* states that Thorfinn "lived usually in Birsay". Nowhere does it say whether this was in the village or on the Brough. It is known locally that south of the parish church, in the village, many substantial walls and settlement debris are to be found, including remains of a Norse hall lying alongside the burn. In the absence of major excavation it is impossible to tell for certain, but there is every possibility that the legacy of Thorfinn's residence, and the land holdings which supported it, could well have been the reason for building the later grand buildings in the village.

Of course, once the remains of the martyred St Magnus had been removed to Kirkwall in the earlier twelfth century, the seat of power of the Earls moved east with them. In time, the bulk of the land ownership in Birsay changed from the Earl to the Church. The area did, however, preserve a high status, continuing to attract Bishops and Earls. A Bishop certainly had or used a palace (named Monsbellus) somewhere in the village in the sixteenth century, and later in this century the Earl's Palace was erected.

It would not be stretching the evidence to suggest that Thorfinn may well have lived in the village, his Christchurch near at hand, with his immediate successors founding a monastery on the Brough which was reliant on the Earl's patronage. The Earl would have been supporting a highly prestigious community, with the added benefit to his soul. The debate continues.

Detail of the ruins which lie under St Magnus Kirk, Birsay – Orkney Library & Archive

Sources and further reading:

Batey C.E., Jesch J.and Morris C.D. (eds) *The Viking Age in Caithness, Orkney and the North Atlantic,* Edinburgh,1993;1995. 67-75

Curle C.L. *The Pictish and Norse Finds from the Brough of Birsay 1934-74* Society of Antiquaries Monograph series No.1 Edinburgh, 1982

Graham-Campbell J. and Batey C.E. *Vikings in Scotland An Archaeological Survey,* Edinburgh, 1998

Graham-Campbell J. et al (eds) *Cultural Atlas of the Viking World* Oxford, 1994

Lowe, C. *St. Boniface Church Orkney Coastal Erosion and Archaeological Assessment,* Stroud,1998

Marwick H *"A Description of Orkney"1773: An Account of an Unpublished Manuscript of Rev. George Low, Minister of Birsay 1774-95* Proc Orkney Antiq Soc, 2 (1924), 49-58

Hunter J.R. *Rescue Excavation on the Brough of Birsay 1972-84,* Society of Antiquaries of Scotland Monograph series No 4, Edinburgh

Lamb R.G. *The Cathedral of Christchurch and the monastery of Birsay* Proc. Soc. Antiq. Scot. 105, 1972-4 200-205

Wainwright F.T. *The Northern Isles* Edinburgh, 1962

Julie Gibson

Marwick Head, Birsay – Raymond Parks

SIGURD THE STOUT AND THE RAVEN BANNER

The events in this chapter take place during the period 991–1014. Earl Sigurd the Stout was the last of the pagan earls of Orkney. With the aid of a magic raven banner he won many battles, but he would fall at the Battle of Clontarf in Ireland as a result of the banner's curse. Several sagas are used to build up a picture of life in Earl Sigurd's court, where raiding was a way of life. Strange tales of supernatural events connected with the Battle of Clontarf are recorded in these sagas, giving it an air of mystery and a brooding sense of doom.

There is much written about Earl Sigurd the Stout, but ironically the account of his life given in the *Orkneyinga Saga* is brief and with little detail. We can fill in the gaps from other sagas, thus giving a much fuller picture of this colourful character.

Sigurd the Stout inherited the earldom of Orkney on the death of his father Earl Hlodver in the year 991. He continued the policy of the occupation of Caithness, much to the king of Scots' dismay. A Scottish earl called Finnleik challenged Earl Sigurd to a battle at Skitten Mire in Caithness to decide the fate of the disputed territory. Sigurd knew that the odds against him were not good; the Scots outnumbered his army seven to one. He went to see his mother Eithne who had the reputation of being a powerful sorceress. Her words to him were contemptuous, saying that if she thought that he could live forever then she would have reared him in her wool-basket. A man's life, she said, was ruled by fate and not by his own actions. After these hard words she brought out a banner and gave it to him. It was richly embroidered with the image of a raven that looked as if it was in flight when the wind blew upon it. She said that she had worked all of her magic into it, so that it would bring victory to the side that bore it, but death to the standard-bearer who held it. Earl Sigurd was angered by his mother's words, but he took the raven banner with him.

Sigurd needed the support of the Orkneymen in the forthcoming battle. He promised to return the odal rights to them that Earl Turf Einar had acquired, if they would support him by raising an army to fight the Scots in Caithness. The promise of becoming freemen once more was a tempting proposition, and the Orkneymen agreed to his terms. The two armies met at Skitten Mire on the appointed day, and Earl Sigurd unfolded his raven banner. The two sides clashed together in a bloody and violent struggle. Sigurd's standard-bearer was shot down, and he ordered another man to take his place. The second standard-bearer also fell, as did a third. By this time Sigurd had defeated the Scottish army, and he held Caithness undisputed after that. The raven was the symbol of Odin, and the standard-bearers were seen as being sacrifices to the god of war in return for victory.

Earl Sigurd went raiding in Scotland and Ireland every year. In 995 he had three longships lying at anchor in Osmundwall in Hoy awaiting favourable tides before setting off on a Viking raid. Here he was surprised by five longships belonging to Olaf Tryggvason, a powerful chieftain returning from exile to claim the throne of Norway. Olaf invited Earl Sigurd over to his ship for talks. The future king of Norway gave Sigurd two choices; he could either agree to be baptized into the Christian faith, or be killed on the spot and the islands be ransacked. Earl Sigurd chose baptism. Olaf took Sigurd's son, called Hundi or Hvelp (hound or whelp) as a hostage, baptizing him with the name Hlodver. He then sailed to Norway with the boy, who died soon after this. After the death of his son Earl Sigurd continued to worship the old gods, and he renounced his allegiance to King Olaf Tryggvason.

Earl Sigurd had three sons called Sumarlidi, Brusi and Einar Wry-mouth. Sigurd would later marry the daughter of King Malcolm of Scotland, who bore him a son called Thorfinn, who would grow up to be the most powerful of the earls of Orkney. The *Orkneyinga Saga* says that Thorfinn the Mighty, as he was later known, extended his realm through Scotland and Ireland.

The *Orkneyinga Saga* has nothing more to say about Earl Sigurd, other than that he died in the Battle of Clontarf in Ireland in 1014. Other sagas give us a picture of life in the court of the Orkney earl, but we must remember that these tales were written long after Sigurd's days and cannot be accepted as facts. Earl Sigurd was a patron of poetry, and a good 'skald' (as poets were called) was a highly respected man. This is shown in the *Saga of Gunnlaug Serpent-tongue*, in which the Icelandic poet Gunnlaug travels to Ireland to the court of King Sigtrygg Silk-beard. He recited a poem in honour of the king, and was rewarded with a suite of scarlet clothes, an embroidered tunic, a fur-lined cloak and a gold bracelet. He then sailed north to Orkney, where he asked Earl Sigurd if he would listen to the poem that he had composed for him. Sigurd said that he would, as Gunnlaug came from such an important family in Iceland. The saga also records that the earl *'... thought highly of Icelanders'*. Gunnlaug recited his poem, much to the delight of Earl Sigurd, and was rewarded with a broad axe, *'decorated all over with silver inlay'*. He was invited to stay for the winter, but he declined as he planned to visit the king of Sweden.

Raiding was an important part of life in the court of Earl Sigurd. In the fragmentary *Thorstein Sidu-Hallsson's Saga* we read that this important Icelander, who was related to Earl Sigurd, arrived in Orkney and stayed with the earl over the winter. In the spring he was asked if he would like to join the earl on a raid, which he immediately agreed to. The saga records the events thus:

> That summer, Earl Sigurd harried across a wide area throughout Scotland, and no one could challenge Thorstein with regard to either valour or temperament… The Earl killed many of the savages, but some fled into the woods. The Vikings pillaged and burned over a wide area in the British Isles. Late in the autumn, the earl went home to the Orkney Islands, and rested there for three months, and then he gave his friends handsome gifts.

Thorstein was given an axe inlaid with gold, which was considered a magnificent gift.

Another piece of evidence for Sigurd's piratical exploits comes from *Eyrbyggja Saga* (The Saga of the People of Eyri). In it we hear how Earl Sigurd had been raiding in the Hebrides and as far south as the Isle of Man:

> He imposed taxes on the inhabitants of Man, and when they had accepted his terms he appointed men to collect the tax, which was paid mainly in refined silver.

An Icelandic trader called Thorodd found a group of people stranded on an uninhabited island off the north coast of Ireland. On investigation he found that they were Earl Sigurd's tax collectors whose ship had been wrecked. They offered him money to take them back to Orkney, because they feared for their lives if the Irish or the Hebrideans captured them as they had just raided their lands. Thorodd could not delay his journey home to Iceland, but he sold them his ship's boat '... *for a large portion of the tax they had collected*'. He was known as Thorodd the Tax-trader after that. It is interesting to note that part of the Viking silver hoard found at Skaill in Sandwick in 1858 was brooches that are thought to have been made in the Isle of Man. It may be stretching things too far to suggest that this silver hoard was part of Earl Sigurd's taxes, but it does suggest that the island was famous for its silver work.

This culture of raiding was a way of gathering wealth, power, and prestige. An earl had to support a lot of warriors, so he needed a large income. In *Vatnsdæla Saga* (The Saga of the People of Vatnsdal) we find a kinsman of Earl Sigurd called Thorkel Scratcher gaining

Hoy in winter – Keith Allardyce

wealth and honour in the earl's court. He was the son of a slave woman, but his father was an important landowner called Thorgrim Hallormsson. When Thorkel was only 12 years old, Thorgrim offered to give him a small axe that he coveted if he would use it to kill a rival of his. Thorkel agreed, and deliberately bumped into the man, who kicked him and called him a slave-woman's son. Thorkel jumped onto the seat next to him and drove the axe into his head. Thorgrim said that the boy was provoked, and that he would now let it be known that he was the boy's father.

Thorkel Scratcher arrived at Earl Sigurd's court where a mutual friend asked the earl to take him in. He made an attempt at telling the earl that they were related, but Sigurd ignored him. He stayed close to the earl, but he was unpopular with the other men. One day in spring the earl's men were competing at games, but Thorkel stayed with the earl. Sigurd asked him to repeat what he had told him about his family. Thorkel told him again of his family, but this time the earl listened to him and realised that they were related. Thorkel's reputation grew, and Earl Sigurd treated him with respect, inviting him to join the next raiding expedition.

On one attack in Scotland the earl asked how many of his men were missing. His men replied that Thorkel was missing, but that he was lazy and of no great loss to them. Earl Sigurd ordered his men to search for him. They found him in a forest clearing fighting with two men, while four others lay dead beside him. The two men ran away when the others arrived. The earl asked what had delayed him, to which Thorkel replied:

Hoy – Raymond Parks

> I have heard you say that men should run from ship to shore; but never that one should run back to the ship in such a way that each man abandons the next.

Earl Sigurd agreed, saying:

> You speak the truth, kinsman, and henceforth this is how things will be; anyone running away from the standard on land shall have no share of the spoils.

The earl then asked who the dead men were, and Thorkel told him that they were natives that he had killed. He said that as he was passing a castle some stones fell from the wall, revealing a large treasure. The men inside the castle had attacked him, and that was how things stood when the earl's men arrived. They recovered the treasure (a large quantity of silver), and Earl Sigurd said that Thorkel should keep it all. Thorkel said that the earl should have it all, but Sigurd decided that they would share it.

Thorkel stayed with Earl Sigurd for two winters before returning to Iceland. The earl thought highly of him, and when he left he gave him a gold-inlaid axe, a fine suit of clothes and a trading ship complete with a cargo of his choice.

Earl Sigurd's death at the Battle of Clontarf in Ireland is vividly told in that great Icelandic classic *Njal's Saga*. The central character of the story, Njal Thorgeirsson, is not the typical warrior hero of sagas, but a man of great wisdom and with the gift of second sight. The saga is an intriguing tale of murder and revenge that weaves its way through the generations. Two of Njal's sons, Helgi and Grim, decide to leave Iceland and travel overseas. The cargo ship they were travelling on was blown south by a gale, then lost in a thick fog. They were attacked by thirteen Viking ships, and despite being hopelessly outnumbered, Helgi and Grim put up a brave fight. They were rescued by Kari Solmundsson who was returning from the Hebrides with ten longships carrying taxes paid to Earl Sigurd. Kari took them to Earl Sigurd who gave them a good welcome and they stayed with the earl over the winter.

As the winter passed, Helgi became quiet and seemed troubled. The earl asked him if there was something wrong and if he was unhappy. Helgi said he was happy, but he asked if the earl had lands to protect in Scotland. Earl Sigurd said that he had, but what of them? Helgi replied that the Scots had killed his man in charge of his Scottish estates and were blocking messages across the Pentland Firth. Earl Sigurd asked if he had second sight, but Helgi said that he had little proof of it. Kari told the earl that Helgi's father had second sight, and that his words would prove to be true. A message was sent to Arnljot, the man in charge of the island of Stroma, and he investigated. He reported that two Scottish earls called Hundi and Melsnati had killed Havard, the earl's brother-in-law, at Freswick in Caithness and that Earl Sigurd should send an army to drive them out. The Njalssons (as Helgi and Grim were known) joined the earl's force and fought fiercely in the battle that took place at Duncansby Head. Earl Melsnati came face to face with Kari and threw his spear at him, but Kari caught the spear in flight and threw it back at Melsnati. The spear passed right through him and he fell dead on the spot. Earl Hundi then fled the battlefield with what remained of the Scots army. Hearing that the Scottish king was gathering a great army, Earl Sigurd spoke with his men and decided that they couldn't possibly win a battle against so many. They retreated to Stroma where they divided the spoils, then returned to the Orkney Mainland. The earl then gave fine gifts to his men. Kari received a sword and a gold-inlaid spear, Helgi a gold bracelet and a cloak, and Grim a sword and shield. The Njalssons went raiding with Kari that summer and spent the following winter with Earl Sigurd. The following spring they sailed to Norway.

They returned to Orkney and spent the winter with Earl Sigurd. Kari and the Njalssons went raiding in Scotland, Wales and the Isle of Man, where they killed Dungal, the son of King Gudrod of Man. They then sailed north to the Hebrides where they stayed with Earl Gilli before returning to Orkney for the winter. Earl Gilli went with them to Orkney where he married Earl Sigurd's sister Nereid. The following summer Kari joined the Njalssons on their voyage home to Iceland and stayed with them at their father's house at Bergthorshvol. The following spring Kari married Njal's daughter Helga, tying himself closer to the family. Helgi and Grim had a brother called Skarphedin, and they were all considered to be great warriors. Feuds led to much bloodshed, culminating in the burning of Njal and his sons in their home. Njal, his wife Bergthora and their sons all died in the blaze, as did Kari's small son Thord. Others died too, but the women were allowed to leave the burning building. Kari was the only one to escape the flames by running up a broken beam with his clothes and hair alight. Helgi Njalsson did manage to get out, but had his head cut off by a man named Flosi. The saga tells of the legal case against the burners, which resulted in Flosi being banished from Iceland for three years and the other burners being banished for life.

Kari killed many of the burners before they left Iceland. Flosi and the remaining burners sailed south in a ship that they had fitted out for the voyage. On the way they were caught up in fog and then lashed by a storm, which wrecked their ship. They struggled ashore with no idea where they were and all their goods had been lost. They climbed a hill to see if they could recognize what land they had come to. One of the men said it was the Orkney Mainland, which troubled Flosi as he knew that Helgi Njalsson was a follower of Earl Sigurd. After hiding for a day Flosi decided that they should go to the earl and surrender themselves. They walked to the earl's hall and greeted him. He knew who they were, as he had already heard about the burning of Njal. The earl asked Flosi what he could tell him about his follower, Helgi Njalsson. Flosi replied that he had struck off his head; this greatly angered the earl who ordered them to be seized. Thorstein Sidu-Hallsson was still staying with the earl and he stepped in to plead for Flosi, who was his brother-in-law. After much pleading by many people the earl made his peace with the burners and he let Flosi replace Helgi as his follower.

Kari had taken a ship south and was staying with a friend in Fridarey (Fair Isle) between Orkney and Shetland. He heard news from the West Mainland that the burners were there with the earl. Earl Sigurd was having a great feast at Yule and he had with him King Sigtrygg

Silk-beard from Ireland and his brother-in-law Earl Gilli from the Hebrides. (*Njal's Saga* contradicts itself at this point, as it says that Earl Gilli was married to Sigurd's sister Hvarflod, yet earlier it called her Nereid.) On Christmas Day 1013 King Sigtrygg and Earl Gilli wanted to hear the story of the burning of Njal, and one of the burners, Gunnar Lambason, was chosen to tell it. He sat in a chair before the guests and began the tale. At the same time Kari arrived outside the hall, and he listened to Gunnar's version of events. Gunnar lied about many things, even claiming that Skarphedin Njalsson wept when the end came. On hearing these lies Kari rushed into the hall and cut off Gunnar's head with one stroke of his sword. The head landed on the table before the king and the earls. Earl Sigurd ordered him to be seized and killed, but nobody rose from their seats. Kari was well liked, and even Flosi said that he had the right to kill Gunnar as he hadn't made peace with the burners. Kari walked from the hall, and Flosi told a true account of the burning.

The reason King Sigtrygg was in Orkney was that he wanted Earl Sigurd's help to defeat King Brian of Ireland. He was accompanied by his mother, Kormlod, who had once been married to King Brian but now wanted him dead. She was a beautiful woman, but with a reputation for being evil. King Sigtrygg offered Earl Sigurd his mother's hand in marriage and his kingdom as well if he would lend his support. Despite opposition from his followers, Sigurd agreed to bring an army to Ireland on Palm Sunday. King Sigtrygg then sought out two Vikings called Brodir and Ospak, who were anchored off the Isle of Man with thirty ships, and tried to enlist their help. He went to see Brodir, a huge man with black hair that was so long he used to tuck it into his belt. He made Brodir the same offer as he made Earl Sigurd, his mother's hand in

Hoy Sound – Keith Allardyce

marriage and his kingdom. Brodir agreed, but Ospak refused to fight King Brian, so they parted company on bad terms, Ospak with ten ships and Brodir with twenty.

These were the events that led up to the Battle of Clontarf that took place near Dublin on Good Friday (23rd April) 1014. The saga writers called it Brian's Battle, and it was seen as a battle between paganism and Christianity. This was not the case, as there were pagans and Christians on both sides. The days leading up to the battle were filled with strange supernatural events. Brodir and his Vikings stayed on board their twenty ships before the battle. One night they were woken by a great noise that filled the air above them, and a shower of boiling blood rained down on them. The men sheltered under their shields, but many were scalded by the blood, which rained down all night until daybreak. The following day they found that one man on every ship had died. The next night the noise returned, but this time swords leapt from their scabbards and spears and axes flew into the air and fought together. The weapons then turned on the men so fiercely that they had a hard time defending themselves and many were wounded, and once more one man on every ship was killed. The third night the noise began again, followed by an attack of ravens with beaks and claws made of iron. The men defended themselves, but again one man on every ship was killed.

The day after this attack Brodir took a boat over to where Ospak's ten ships lay anchored inside a bay. Ospak was a pagan, but was considered to be a wise man. Brodir told him of the previous three nights' events and asked him what it meant. Ospak didn't trust Brodir, as he

North Ronaldsay sheep on beach, North Ronaldsay – Raymond Parks

knew that he would act violently if he was told something that he did not want to hear, but he knew that he never killed at night, so he delayed answering him until sunset. He then told Brodir that the boiling blood signified that he would shed much blood, both his own and other people's. The terrible noise meant that he would witness the breaking-up of the world, and would die soon. The weapons fighting by themselves meant that he would take part in a great battle, and the ravens represented the demons that would carry him off to Hell. Brodir was furious at this interpretation of the events, and ordered his ships to block the mouth of the bay so that he could attack Ospak when it was light. Ospak had the ropes that secured Brodir's ships cut, and escaped to Ireland where he told King Brian of the coming battle and accepted baptism from him.

Earl Sigurd gathered together his warriors from Orkney and made ready to sail to Ireland. Flosi offered to go, but was refused, as he had sworn to make a pilgrimage to Rome. Fifteen of Flosi's men sailed with the earl. Thorstein Sidu-Hallsson also sailed with Earl Sigurd. The earl refused the offer of assistance from a man called Harek, but he promised him that he would be the first to know the outcome. They arrived in Dublin on Palm Sunday. Brodir and his men were already there. He had once been a Christian and was a consecrated mass-deacon, but had rejected the faith and become a sorcerer instead. Brodir predicted that if they were to fight on Good Friday then King Brian would be killed but would still win the victory; if they fought before Friday they would all be killed. Brodir declared that they should not fight before Friday. King Brian had gathered an army, and marched out to meet King Sigtrygg on Good Friday. Brian did not want to fight on such a holy day, and stayed at the back behind a shield wall.

Brodir was on one flank of the army, King Sigtrygg on the other, and Earl Sigurd was in the centre with his magic raven banner. When the two sides clashed, Brodir cut his way through the warriors until he was attacked by King Brian's brother, Ulf (wolf) Hraeda. Ulf knocked Brodir on his back three times, causing him to run for cover in the woods. Earl Sigurd's men were attacked by Kerthjalfad, the foster-son of King Brian. He cut his way through them right up to the raven banner and killed the standard bearer. Sigurd ordered another man to pick up the banner, but Kerthjalfad killed this standard bearer too. Earl Sigurd ordered Thorstein Sidu-Hallsson to pick up the banner, but as *Njal's Saga* says:

> Then Amundi the White said, "Don't take the banner; everybody who does gets killed"
>
> "Hrafn the Red," said the earl, "you carry the banner."
>
> "Carry that devilish thing yourself," answered Hrafn.
>
> The earl said, "Then it's best that the beggar and his bag go together," and he took the banner off the pole and stuck it between his clothes. A little later, Amundi the White was killed. Then the earl was pierced through by a spear.

Earl Sigurd's death is also recorded in *Thorstein Sidu-Hallsson's Saga*, although the players differ from *Njal's Saga*:

Three of the earl's standard-bearers fell there, and the earl asked Thorstein to carry the standard.

"You carry your own raven, earl," Thorstein replied.

Then a man said, "You're doing the right thing, Thorstein: I've lost three of my sons because of it."

The earl took the flag off the pole and tucked it into his clothes and then fought very bravely. A little later, they heard a voice from the sky:

"If Earl Sigurd wants victory, he should make for Dumasbakki with his men."

Thorstein always followed the earl, and he did so once more then. The earl died in that attack, and his followers were scattered in all directions.

Njal's Saga records how Thorstein's life was saved when he stopped to tie his shoe-string while the other followers of Earl Sigurd fled. He was asked by King Brian's foster-son Kerthjalfad why he wasn't running away:

Because I can't reach home tonight – my home's out in Iceland.

Kerthjalfad spared his life and Thorstein returned to Orkney.

Hoy Cliffs – Raymond Parks

Ospak the Viking fought against King Sigtrygg's army so fiercely that they eventually scattered and fled the battlefield. King Brian's men chased their vanquished foes, leaving the king with only a few guards. Brodir was still hiding in the woods, and he saw that Brian was exposed. He charged at the shield wall and cut his way through it and killed King Brian in the very hour of his victory. Ulf Hraeda and Kerthjalfad turned back and surrounded Brodir and his men. They used branches to push against them so that they could be captured alive. All of Brodir's men were killed and Ulf decided Brodir's death. He cut open Brodir's belly and fastened his intestines to an oak tree and then led him around it until all his guts were drawn out. Brodir only died when all his intestines were pulled from his body.

Njal's Saga also contains one of the strangest stories ever told in a saga. On the morning of Good Friday, a man in Caithness named Dorrud saw twelve people riding to a woman's workroom, where they went inside. He went and looked through the window and saw that all the people were women, and that they had set up a loom. These were no ordinary women and it was no ordinary loom either. The uprights were made of spears, the loom-weights were men's heads and the cloth was woven from human entrails. Swords were used as weaving battens and arrows served as shuttles. As they wove this gory cloth the women chanted verses over it. These women were the valkyries, the handmaidens of Odin, who decide who dies in battle, and who choose the warriors that will go to Valhalla. As they wove they were directing the fate of the warriors and the battle itself. When they had finished they tore the cloth from the loom and each one took a part with them, six going to the north and six to the south.

Earl Sigurd's faithful follower Harek waited in Orkney for news of the battle. One day he saw Earl Sigurd and some of his men returning, and he took a horse and rode to meet them. People saw them meet, then Harek went with Earl Sigurd and his men and they disappeared behind a hill. Nobody ever saw Harek again, nor the ghostly army of Earl Sigurd the Stout.

WESTNESS, ROUSAY

Packed into a couple of kilometres of shore is a range of evidence for what happened when the Vikings took over Orkney in the eighth and ninth centuries, as well as for the time of the Sagas when Sigurd of Westness farmed the lands here.

The Pictish village at Midhowe, Westness, flourished in the ditches and ruins of the crumbling broch. The sea has taken an unknown amount of this village, but round the back of broch, in the ditch, snuggle several buildings. Each house consisted of several small rooms, most with central hearths, round a courtyard area. Each room probably supported its own roof, thus creating a very cosy environment. Exceptionally neat stonework, little built-in cupboards and handy stairs up to the ramparts of the ditch add to this impression of comfort. It is worth taking a moment to imagine the people in amongst these rooms, for these are the people the Vikings encountered when they started their spring and autumn raids before finally, according to the saga *Historia Norwegiae*, wiping out all who were left.

The warriors on the Birsay symbol stone are carrying spears and shields. Their shields are highly decorated, and their clothes are also evidently rather beautifully woven with bands and fringes, reflecting the importance of the men portrayed. Although the context of portraiture on a symbol stone is about as formal as one could get, their appearance is confirmed by other found objects, not made to impress. The oldest garment in Scotland is a Pictish hood, discovered perfectly preserved in a bog in Tankerness, Orkney. This child's garment, cut down and remade from worn adult garments, is also highly decorative and heavily fringed from shoulder to waist. The flamboyant "curlers-left-in" hairstyle sported by the Birsay warriors is also to be seen portrayed on a piece of graffiti from Jarlshof, Shetland. Archaeological evidence from Birsay and particularly Mine Howe demonstrates that the Picts were expert metalworkers. Their interest in portable and showy wealth would no doubt have made them prime targets for Viking pirates. It seems Pictish life, before the Vikings, might have been rather a pleasant affair.

Although the Pictish sphere of influence covers about a third of Scotland, there is no evidence that Orkney commanded any centralised force to respond to Viking incursions. On the contrary, because Orkney and Shetland would have been fringe territory to the Picts, and because each consists of many small islands, Viking war bands, becoming very familiar with the territory, could have picked off the island Picts bit by bit. This probably results in different histories of this in different places in the islands.

The graves at the point of Moaness, Westness were first discovered in the 1960s by accident. A farm worker burying a cow came across the grave of a rich, obese, Viking woman who had died in childbirth. She had been buried with her antique Irish brooch, decorated in gold and enamels, and many other goods for her afterlife. Later, it was discovered that she had been buried in a much larger cemetery, of more than 30 graves. These graves represented a mixture of Picts and Vikings. All the Pictish graves were dug as extended east-west inhumations, with no grave goods. Some, but not all the bodies were laid in stone cists. The graves of this style have been dated to between the fifth and late seventh centuries. The Picts *may* have been Christian. Certainly they were buried in a Christian style; their graves were created on an east-west axis and no grave goods accompanied the bodies. No chapel or church was found, although this is no evidence either way, since coastal erosion is very active here, and it is entirely possible that any chapel may have gone. No cross-incised stones have been found. Negative evidence is not good evidence, however. It is, conversely,

Aerial view of Westness – Richard Welsby

entirely possible that these Picts may have been pagan. Throughout the Pictish period here, the graves maintain a similar layout and style; it is not possible, therefore, to see a conversion to Christianity marked by any difference in practice, during the life of this cemetery. Thus, either Westness was a very early conversion, or perhaps this was a pagan cemetery. Later, the Vikings started to bury their dead in the same area. Several different styles of pagan Viking burial were found here, from men buried in their old fishing boats with their swords, shields, and other goods to men and women in simpler oval graves accompanied perhaps only by a sickle or knife and comb. One of the Vikings had apparently met a violent end; arrows were found embedded in the bones of his body. One of the Viking graves had been robbed in antiquity, but interestingly none of the Pictish ones seem to have been disturbed by the later Viking burials. This "respect" is often adduced as evidence that the Viking take-over of Orkney was a peaceable affair. It should be noted, though, that burials in the extended or long-cist style do not continue in this cemetery into the Viking time period, and this would offer evidence to the contrary.

The geography of Orkney was well known to the writers of the *Orkneyinga Saga*, and this veracity was clearly necessary as the background to a series of stories about events, for these events to be believable. When visiting Westness, for instance, it is very tempting to try to locate exactly where Earl Paul was ambushed by Svein Asleifsson, or to try to identify the spot where Sigurd would have had his hall. There are three candidates for the exact spot where Sigurd of Westness lived. These are: under the present day Westness farm; at an unnamed longhouse site on the bay near Sweindro; or at the Wirk, a site near to the church.

Near the cemetery of Moaness, near Sweindro, the foundations of a farmstead can still be seen. Shortened to an unknown extent by the incursions of the sea, the long-house extends from under the storm beach, where it was not excavated, back to the edge of the bog behind. It consists of a divided hall of three rooms with a total length of some 35m. Inside, the rooms had long hearths, some with side benches. The excavated rooms were dated to the twelfth century. They are thus contemporary with Sigurd of Westness. Beside the house, and contemporary with it, was a byre, which was built parallel to the house, end on to the shore, and connected by a narrow paved yard. This would have made it easier to attend dry-shod to the eighteen cattle and sheep which would have been indoors in the winter. Although quite substantial and quite probably contemporary with him, the amount of wealth commanded at this house (as represented by the reasonably modest byre) does not seem adequate to support the *Orkneyinga Saga* figure, Sigurd of Westness. So probably we should look for his hall elsewhere in this area.

The reason that Earl Paul is at Westness is because, being a medieval prince, he is partly maintained through the hospitality given to him and his retinue by visits to his aristocratic supporters. Sigurd of Westness is closely related by marriage to Earl Paul, and is thus entertaining him, in this way - as the Saga says, "*i veizlu*".

A man of Sigurd's status would have needed a chapel close by, and St Mary's is the only candidate on the Westside of Rousay. The farm at Westness has no known or suspected chapel site. Therefore at Westness, the area near the church is the most likely place for Sigurd's hall. There are several reasons backing this supposition. Firstly the place-name *Skaill* comes from the Old Norse *Skali* meaning hall. As a place name it has high status connotations. As in this case, in Orkney, many *Skaills* are in close proximity to chapels which become the parish church. The present church has been re-built, post-Reformation, but several pieces of decorated red sandstone can be seen in the re-build, and several more of these architectural fragments, which came from the church, are now to be seen built into a garden gate at Trumland House. These fragments are probably thirteenth century; that is a hundred years later than Sigurd, but they confirm the high status of the site. It is therefore almost certain that Sigurd lived nearby.

In the 1930s excavations were undertaken by J.Storer Clouston, an Orcadian antiquarian, as part of his long-running search for solid evidence for Saga sites. At the corner of the present churchyard he discovered the remains of a substantial house (also thirteenth or fourteenth century). This would have been a building like a smaller version of the Bishop's

A carved stone from the Wirk – Orkney Library & Archive

or Earl's palaces in Kirkwall – with grand hall upstairs, and kitchens below. This building, called the Wirk, was attached to a small square tower, the remains of which can be seen today.

Of course a high status building is a clue that we are looking in the right area, but the building is a minimum of 100 years too late for Sigurd. Could the tower alone be Sigurd's? As always the evidence requires some interpretation. The building style of long straight stones is often compared with Cubbie Roo's castle, in Wyre. Therefore it is thought that this might be Sigurd's equivalent retreat. Clouston thought it was possibly a separate church tower, which could have been used by Sigurd in times of danger. Most recently it has become accepted that the shoots (chutes) visible in the stonework mean that this was a garderobe (or toilet) tower, in use with the hall.

The view that this represents the original purpose of the tower may yet be up for discussion, for in this author's opinion it is more likely that the tower started life as part of a small fortlet created by Sigurd of Westness, or his immediate descendants. The sagas make it clear that "might" was pretty much "right" in Saga times. Cubbie Roo or *Kolbein Hruga* in Wyre required a very substantial castle. The sagas also refer to a *kastali* in Damsay. The place-name Brough, now attached to a nearby farmstead of the eighteenth and nineteenth centuries is a reference to some sort of fortification. Also, since the Iron Age brochs in the area are called by reference to their ruins North, Mid and South Howe, this could well refer to another type of *borg*. Raymond Lamb has drawn attention to documentation of the sixteenth century which refers to the "house and fortalice at Brough" which is probably the Wirk, but which once again refers to some kind of fortification. Sigurd of Westness had to put up with the so-called *last of the Vikings* Svein Asleifsson, as a neighbour. He would have needed to fortify his house in some way, and it seems very likely this was it.

We can, perhaps, also see Sigurd as the owner of the noust at Moaness? Here, near the site of the pagan graves, in the twelfth century a large boat house stood on the shore. The foundations are still visible today. Stone built, three-sided, with open end to the sea, there is a cobbled ramp at the inland end for an ox or horse to be harnessed, to help tow a boat ashore. This bay is the first one (coming from the West) in which it is sheltered enough to moor a boat. Standing in the foundations of the boat house, and looking directly through the open end out to sea at low tide, one can clearly see how the rocks have been cleared or cut back to facilitate a boat's

Excavations at the Wirk – Orkney Library & Archive

Scabra Head – Max Fletcher

landing. This boat house could have covered a substantial cargo boat or warship. The *Orkneyinga Saga* relates a story that probably involves just such a boat. The story goes that Svein Asleifsson was coming back from raiding in the Western Isles, through Eynhallow Sound. Other men might have thought to go straight home, when it was so close. But Svein, having an eye to the main chance and spotting Earl Paul hunting otters on the rocks below the cliffs of Westness, decided to chance his luck. He got his men to hide below the leather covers of the cargo, therefore looking more like merchant men than a raiding party. Earl Paul signalled them to come ashore, thus inviting his own end. Svein and his men came ashore out of sight of the Earl, and subsequently ambushed him. They killed several of his retainers and kidnapped the Earl. Just as it was Sigurd's duty to raise the levy of men from Rousay, Raymond Lamb has pointed out that it is likely that Sigurd would also have needed to contribute a warship. So, in these foundations, perhaps we can indeed see something of Sigurd's legacy.

Julie Gibson

Further Reading: Downes J and Ritchie A, 2003, *Sea Change Orkney and Northern Europe in the Later Iron Age AD 300-800.*

Kaland, SHH, 1993 "The settlement of Westness, Rousay" in Batey, CE, Jesch,J and Morris CD (eds) 1993 The Viking Age in Caithness, Orkney and the North Atlantic, Edinburgh.

Skipigeo – Raymond Parks

EARL THORFINN THE MIGHTY

The events in this chapter take place during the period 1014–1066. Earl Thorfinn the Mighty was only a child when his father Earl Sigurd the Stout died in battle. His older half-brothers refused to share the earldom of Orkney with Thorfinn, who had already been granted the earldoms of Caithness and Sutherland by his grandfather, King Malcolm of Scotland. Here for the first time we have an earl of Orkney whose loyalty was split between the King of Scots and the King of Norway. Earl Thorfinn's greed for power and territory was aided by his foster-father, Thorkel Fosterer. Thorkel's murder of Earl Einar gave Thorfinn the opportunity to seize control of territory in Orkney. When Earl Thorfinn had to share power with his nephew Earl Rognvald it inevitably turned to bloodshed. When Earl Rognvald fell into the hands of Earl Thorfinn's men, it is again the faithful Thorkel Fosterer who carries out the killing. Earl Thorfinn the Mighty extended his territory deep into Scotland, the Hebrides and Ireland; further than any other earl of Orkney. His two sons, Paul and Erlend, fought for the Norwegian King Harald Hard-ruler at Stamford Bridge in 1066 when King Harald and his warriors were massacred by the English army under King Harold Godwinsson. This battle effectively brought the Viking age to a close.

Dingieshowe from shore – Orkney Library & Archive

Most of the saga references to Earl Thorfinn the Mighty come from the *Orkneyinga Saga*, with some extra information from *Heimskringla*. It is interesting to note that Snorri Sturluson has quoted a whole section from the early form of the *Orkneyinga Saga* (called the *Jarlasaga*) in *Heimskringla*. It records the history of the early earls up to Thorfinn's visit to King Olaf the Saint after the killing of Earl Einar (see below), and is almost word for word the same. It is known that Snorri had a copy of this prototype of the *Orkneyinga Saga*, and used it as a reference while writing his sagas of the kings of Norway that make up *Heimskringla*.

Earl Sigurd the Stout's three eldest sons, Sumarlidi, Brusi and Einar, ruled Orkney after their father's death at the Battle of Clontarf in 1014. They split the earldom into three parts and each ruled their own third. Earl Sigurd had another son, Thorfinn, who was only five when his father died. He was being raised at the court of the Scottish King Malcolm II, who was his grandfather. King Malcolm granted Thorfinn the earldoms of Caithness and Sutherland and appointed regents to rule there until he was old enough to take control.

Sumarlidi was the eldest of Earl Sigurd the Stout's sons, and the shortest lived. He died in his bed not long after his father's death. Thorfinn now claimed Sumarlidi's third of the earldom for himself, but Einar refused, saying that Thorfinn already held Caithness and Sutherland, which had belonged to Earl Sigurd, and that was more than a third of the earldom. Earl Einar was a great bully, a hard and ambitious man who differed from his mild-mannered brother Earl Brusi. People called him Einar Wry-mouth. Thorfinn would grow up to be a tall and strong man, ugly and with sharp features, a big nose and black hair. He too was greedy and ambitious,

Drawing of Old Kirk, Skaill, 1774 – Rev. Low – Orkney Library & Archive

like his half-brother Einar. Brusi said that he didn't want Sumarlidi's third of the earldom, as he was happy with his own share. Earl Einar took over the vacant third of the earldom as well as his own portion. He was an overbearing ruler, and demanded both taxes and men to support his raiding expeditions. This resulted in a bad harvest for the farmers who lived in Earl Einar's two thirds of the islands, while Earl Brusi's farmers enjoyed a good harvest.

Around 1016–18 there was a farmer named Amundi, who lived at Hlaupandanes in Deerness, probably on the site of the modern farm of Skaill. Earl Einar Wry-mouth called a 'Thing,' an assembly of the local farmers, which probably took place at the great mound at Dingieshowe. He was going to ask for his usual high level of taxes, but the farmers were not happy. They appealed to Amundi to speak on their behalf and plead for a reduction in taxes. Amundi refused, so the farmers made the same plea to his son Thorkel. He agreed to speak for them, and he pleaded their case in front of the earl. Earl Einar said that he had intended to take six ships with him to go raiding that spring, but now he would take only three. He warned Thorkel never to ask him for a concession again. Einar Wry-mouth returned that autumn, but the following spring he made another demand for taxes from the farmers. They again persuaded Thorkel to speak on their behalf, but this time Earl Einar grew furious and said that the farmers would suffer for their plea, and that another spring would not see both himself and Thorkel there safe and sound. Amundi urged his son to leave Orkney, and Thorkel sailed to safety in Caithness. He was taken in by the young Earl Thorfinn, whom he fostered, gaining himself the name Thorkel Fosterer.

When Thorfinn came of age he asked Earl Einar for the third of the islands that had belonged to Sumerlidi. Einar refused to give up any land, so Thorfinn gathered an army in Caithness and sailed to Orkney. Earl Einar gathered together an army in Orkney to defend his territory and went to meet Earl Thorfinn. Earl Brusi also raised a body of men and went between them to try to forge a peace treaty. It was resolved that Thorfinn should have the disputed third, while Einar and Brusi would share the other two thirds with Einar as overlord with responsibility for defence. It was decided that when one of the two brothers died, the survivor would take control of the two thirds. This was thought unfair, as Brusi had a son called Rognvald, while Einar had no sons.

Earl Thorfinn had stewards appointed to rule his estate in Orkney while he continued to live in Caithness. Earl Einar Wry-mouth would go raiding in Ireland, Scotland and Wales every year. In the summer of 1017 he fought a battle with King Konofogar (Conchobhar) at Lough Larne in Ireland and suffered a great defeat. *Heimskringla* records that Einar escaped in just one ship and that he lost almost all of his men and all of his booty. The following summer a Norwegian chieftain called Eyvind Urus-horn[7] was forced to shelter in Osmundwall as he tried to sail through the Pentland Firth. Eyvind had fought against Earl Einar in Ireland, and once the earl heard that he was sheltering in Orkney he raised a great force and captured him. Einar had Eyvind put to death, but he spared his men, who went to Norway and told King Olaf what had happened. The king said little about the killing, but he took the death of his follower personally.

---

[7] Aurochs-horn. An aurochs was an ancient breed of wild cow.

Earl Thorfinn sent Thorkel Fosterer to Orkney to collect his taxes. Earl Einar Wry-mouth blamed Thorkel for encouraging Earl Thorfinn to lay claim to his third of Orkney and he drove him from the islands. Thorfinn advised him to leave the country and go to King Olaf in Norway. The king noticed that Thorkel was full of praise for Earl Thorfinn, but had little good to say about Earl Einar. Thorfinn was invited to Norway as a guest of the king, and sailed there in the summer of 1020. On the way back, they landed in Orkney and were met by Earl Einar with an army. Earl Brusi again made peace between the two half-brothers, and it was agreed that Thorkel Fosterer and Earl Einar should entertain each other to a feast as a gesture of friendship.

In October 1020 Earl Einar Wry-mouth went to Thorkel's hall at Hlaupandanes in Deerness where a grand feast and strong drink was served. Einar was not in a happy mood during his time there. It then came to be Earl Einar's turn to entertain Thorkel Fosterer and they made ready to leave together. Thorkel didn't trust Einar and had spies search the route they were to take. They reported that there were three separate groups of armed men waiting to ambush Thorkel along the road. Earl Einar was growing angry because of the delay in leaving and he sat by the fire in the great hall. Thorkel walked in through one of the doors, which was closed behind him by an Icelander from the East Fjords called Hallvard. They walked up to Earl Einar, who asked if they were not ready yet. *'I am ready now,'* replied Thorkel, and struck Einar on the head. The earl fell dead into the fire. Hallvard the Icelander rebuked the earl's men for not pulling him out of the fire and he drove the curve of his axe into the earl's neck and hauled his body up onto the benches. The two of them then ran out through another door where Thorkel's men were waiting fully armed. Earl Einar's men were so shocked that they took away the body and never offered to put up a fight. Thorkel sailed to Norway where King Olaf gave him a warm welcome.

Earl Brusi now had control of two-thirds of Orkney, as had been agreed with Earl Einar. Earl Thorfinn was too greedy to let the agreement stand, and he asked Earl Brusi for half of the islands. Brusi knew that he couldn't fight Thorfinn, so in the spring of 1021 he sailed to Norway to ask for support from the king. King Olaf now claimed that the Norwegian kings had sovereignty over the islands and forced Brusi to acknowledge his right to appoint whomever he wanted as earl. Brusi was in no position to argue and surrendered his two-thirds of the islands to the king. Earl Thorfinn followed Earl Brusi to Norway in an attempt to secure his claim. Thorfinn was also forced to acknowledge King Olaf's right to the islands and swear loyalty to him. Thorfinn was reluctant at first, because he said that he was already a follower of the Scottish king. Thorkel Fosterer had sent a message to Earl Thorfinn warning him to accept the king's terms, which he eventually did. King Olaf decided that they should have their third share each, but that he would claim the third portion in compensation for Earl Einar's killing of his friend and follower Eyvind Urus-horn. Thorkel was reconciled with the two earls for the killing of their brother and he remained with Earl Thorfinn afterwards.

Earl Thorfinn returned home as quickly as he could, but Earl Brusi stayed behind. King Olaf told Brusi that he would grant him the last third of Orkney to rule on the king's behalf. King Olaf asked Brusi to leave his son, Rognvald, behind in Norway. He was only ten years old at the time, but was already large for his age and would grow into a tall, strong man with long golden silk-like hair. He was raised by the king as his foster-son. Earl Brusi did not enjoy his two-thirds of the earldom for long. Earl Thorfinn did nothing to defend Orkney and Shetland from raiders, but he still collected taxes from the islands. When Earl Brusi complained, Earl Thorfinn made him an offer: that he would defend all of the islands in return for the third of the earldom that had belonged to Earl Einar. Brusi accepted, and Thorfinn took over two-thirds of the islands.

Earl Thorfinn's grandfather, King Malcolm II of Scotland, was murdered in the year 1034 and was replaced by a man called Karl Hundisson.[8] Because this name translates as 'peasant son of a dog', we can assume that it wasn't his real name. King Karl Hundisson claimed Caithness as his property and demanded that Earl Thorfinn should pay him taxes. Thorfinn refused, and hostilities broke out between them. The Scottish king appointed his own earl over Caithness, but this earl was attacked by Thorkel Fosterer who set fire to his house and beheaded him when he leapt from an upstairs balcony. The situation came to a head when King Karl Hundisson raised a huge army from Scotland and Ireland and met Earl Thorfinn at Tarbat Ness on the Moray Firth. Thorfinn was outnumbered, but, wearing a gilded helmet and wielding a great spear, Thorfinn drove on his men to victory. Some say that Karl Hundisson was killed during the battle. Earl Thorfinn continued south, killing and burning as he went. He returned home to Caithness and lived there during the winter but continued to raid throughout Britain and Ireland during the rest of the year. Earl Brusi died in the early 1030s and Thorfinn took control of all of Orkney.

[8] King Malcolm II was actually replaced by King Duncan I.

Composite picture of Osmundwall, Hoy – Anne Brundle

The situation in Norway during this period was extremely unstable, as we can read in *Heimskringla*. Knut the Mighty, the king of Denmark and England, sent messengers to King Olaf in 1025 claiming the crown of Norway for himself. He argued that his forefathers had ruled Norway and it was part of his kingdom, but he would retain Olaf as an earl who could gather taxes on his behalf. King Olaf refused, but he was driven out of Norway by Knut's huge army. In 1028 King Knut placed Hakon the Jarl (earl) in control of the country, supported by many powerful chieftains and their bonders, as the farmers were known. Rognvald Brusisson was in his late teens by this time, and he shared exile in Russia with his foster-father King Olaf.

Olaf returned to Norway in 1030 in an attempt to regain his kingdom. Unwilling to face more years of civil war the bonders raised a great army, led by many powerful chieftains that Olaf had fallen out with. Among those chiefs were Tore the Hound from Northern Norway, whose nephew had been killed by Olaf, and Kalf Arnisson, who was the uncle of Earl Thorfinn's wife Ingibjorg. Ingibjorg's father, Finn Arnisson, fought with King Olaf in the coming battle. The bonders' army gathered for battle at Stiklestad, north of Trondheim, and were met there by King Olaf's army. The meeting of the two armies had portents of doom for Olaf, as recorded in a book of sagas from Iceland known as the *Flatteyarbok*:

St Boniface Kirk, Papa Westray – Vicki Szabo

> Where they were standing there were berries on a mound. The king takes the berries and squeezes them in his palm. Then the king saw where the banner of the freemen was set up. Then he spoke and said, "Wretched berries," quoth he. Rognvald Brusisson answers, "You made a slip of the tongue just now, king, you must have meant to say 'people.'" "Thou sayest right, earl," quoth the king, "Thou will not make a less slip of the tongue when thou hast but a short time to live." That happened afterwards, as is said in the Earls' Saga.[9]

Heimskringla states that King Olaf's young half-brother, Harald Sigurdsson (later King Harald the Hard-ruler), was among his followers. King Olaf wanted Harald to leave the battlefield, as he was still only a boy of around fifteen, but Harald argued that he would bind his hand to his sword hilt in order to swing it even if he grew tired. Olaf accepted, and Harald fought in the battle. King Olaf wore a golden helmet and carried a white shield with a gold cross painted on it. Both sides prepared for battle, which took place on Wednesday 29th July, 1030. King Olaf struck Tore the Hound with his sword, but it did not penetrate his reindeer cloak, which was protected by sorcery. Thorstein the Shipwright struck King Olaf on the left leg above the knee with his axe. This wound caused King Olaf to lean against a large rock for support. Finn Arnisson (brother of Kalf Arnisson and the father-in-law of Earl Thorfinn) attacked Thorstein the Shipwright and killed him. Meanwhile Tore the Hound thrust his spear up under the king's chain mail 'brynie' and into his stomach. Kalf Arnisson struck the king on the left side of his neck with his axe, causing his death. (People at the time argued that it was in fact Kalf Arnisson's kinsman Kalf Arnfinnsson who had dealt this lethal blow.) With the death of King Olaf his army broke up and many fled, leaving the bonders' army victorious. Kalf Arnisson found his brothers, Finn and Torberg, lying on the battlefield exhausted. Finn threw his sword at his brother Kalf in an attempt to kill him, and he cursed him as a betrayer of his king. Kalf had his brothers removed to the safety of a ship and sailed away from the battlefield.

The *Orkneyinga Saga* tells how Rognvald Brusisson had also survived the battle and had found Harald Sigurdsson lying wounded on the battlefield. Being King Olaf's half-brother, Harald's life was in danger should he be discovered, and so Rognvald rescued him and brought him to a bonder's house that was hidden away in the woods. Here he was looked after until he was well enough to travel. Rognvald, along with his foster-brother Magnus (the son of King Olaf), travelled to Sweden where Harald Sigurdsson joined them later. King Olaf's wife, Queen Astrid, was the daughter of King Olaf of Sweden and it was she who took them in. Magnus was not Astrid's son, but the illegitimate son of Olaf and a woman called Alvhild, who had been Queen Astrid's serving maid. They then went from Sweden to King Jaroslav in Novgorod, Russia, who received them well. King Jaroslav was married to Queen Astrid's sister, Ingegerd, who was at one time betrothed to King Olaf. Harald Sigurdsson went south to Constantinople (Istanbul) and served as a bodyguard to the Emperor. Rognvald Brusisson remained in Novgorod where he served in the defence of the land, fighting in ten battles.

Finding that Danish rule in Norway was harsher than expected, Kalf Arnisson travelled to Novgorod to find Magnus Olafsson and offer to raise an army in Norway to put him on his

---

[9] From appendix to G.W. Dasent's translation of Orkneyinga Saga, 1894.

father's throne. Rognvald saw Kalf in Ladoga, and, filled with rage, he was about to attack him before he was stopped by Einar Bowstring-shaker, who had travelled with Kalf. He told Rognvald the reason for their journey and asked Rognvald to come with them to King Jaroslav and help plead their case. King Jaroslav was not keen to allow Magnus to go with the man who had killed his father, but in the end he was persuaded to allow him to leave. Kalf and Einar returned to Norway to prepare the way for Magnus to be accepted as king. Rognvald accompanied the eleven-year-old Magnus to Norway in 1035, where he was accepted as king, becoming known as King Magnus the Good. His father, King Olaf, was now considered to be a saint, and became the patron saint of Norway.

While Rognvald was in Norway, he heard the news that his father, Earl Brusi, had died and that his uncle Earl Thorfinn now ruled all of the islands. He asked King Magnus for permission to go to Orkney to claim his inheritance. King Magnus granted him the title of earl, and gave him his father's third of the islands, along with the disputed third that King Olaf had claimed. King Magnus gave Rognvald three longships fully fitted out for war, and he sailed to his father's estate in Orkney. Messengers were sent to Earl Thorfinn asking him to give up the two-thirds of the islands to his nephew, Rognvald Brusisson. Thorfinn was having trouble keeping his growing earldom under control, because there were uprisings in the Hebrides and Ireland. He said that he would give Rognvald his third as his birthright, and he was willing to let him have the king's third if he would support him in battle. Rognvald agreed, and took control of two-thirds of the earldom. Earl Rognvald and Earl Thorfinn went raiding together and all was well for eight years. Rognvald lived in Orkney while Thorfinn lived mostly in Caithness. It was Earl Rognvald Brusisson who had a church built and dedicated to his foster-father, Saint Olaf, in the small trading village of Kirkwall.

Back in Norway, King Magnus the Good had fallen out with his father's killer, Kalf Arnisson, who fled to Earl Thorfinn. Thorfinn was married to Kalf's niece, making him a kinsman of the earl. Kalf Arnisson was accompanied by a great number of men and Earl Thorfinn had to bear the expense of keeping them in food and drink. People started to urge Earl Thorfinn to claim back the disputed third of the island from Earl Rognvald, as Thorfinn had so many warriors to support. Messengers were sent to Orkney to ask Rognvald to give up that third of the islands that had belonged to Earl Einar Wry-mouth. Rognvald refused this request, saying it was King Magnus's property to dispose of as he saw fit. Earl Thorfinn was furious and raised a huge army from his earldoms in Scotland to fight Earl Rognvald for the disputed third of Orkney. Rognvald could not raise enough warriors from his two-thirds share of the islands to take on and fight Thorfinn's army. Instead he sailed east to Norway and appealed to King Magnus to raise an army to fight on his behalf. King Magnus agreed, and also offered to forgive Kalf Arnisson and return his estates to him in Norway if he took Earl Rognvald's side in the forthcoming battle.

Earl Rognvald sailed west to Shetland around the year 1046 and gathered men to fight against Earl Thorfinn. He then sailed south to Orkney and gained support from his friends there. When Thorfinn heard this he raised another army from Scotland and the Hebrides and prepared to sail to Orkney and fight Rognvald. Earl Rognvald had gathered thirty large ships and set sail into the Pentland Firth on the way to Caithness. Somewhere off Hoy, they met Earl Thorfinn with a force of sixty ships, but they were all small vessels. Rognvald's larger ships had the advantage, and soon Thorfinn was losing men. Kalf Arnisson had arrived with six large ships, but Rognvald had conveyed the message of peace from King Magnus to Kalf, who kept out of the fighting. Seeing that his position was precarious, Thorfinn rowed his ship to Kalf Arnisson and urged him to fight on his behalf. He said that if Rognvald gained control in the west then Kalf would find himself in a dangerous position should his friendship with King Magnus fail again. Kalf Arnisson ordered his men to attack Rognvald's smallest ships. Earl Thorfinn rowed his ship against Earl Rognvald's vessel and a bitter fight broke out. Kalf helped to turn the tables in Thorfinn's favour, forcing Rognvald to cut the grappling ropes and flee east to Norway.

Thorfinn now claimed all of Orkney and had all the people there swear an oath of allegiance to him. Earl Rognvald lived with King Magnus until the winter, when he decided to have one more attempt to defeat Earl Thorfinn. King Magnus offered him as many ships and men as he wanted, but Rognvald declined the offer, saying that Thorfinn's army was too great to defeat by force alone. Instead he asked for a single ship and a handpicked crew. If he was to win the earldom, it would be by surprise. Earl Rognvald sailed to Shetland where he heard that Earl Thorfinn was in Orkney and had only a small band of warriors with him, because he wasn't expecting an attack in midwinter. Rognvald sailed swiftly to the Orkney Mainland and surrounded the house where Thorfinn was staying. Rognvald's men secured the doors and then set fire to the house. Thorfinn was still sitting up drinking, while his men slept.

Hog-back stone, St Boniface Kirk, Papa Westray – Vicki Szabo

He sent men to the door to ask who the attackers were, and was told that it was Earl Rognvald. Earl Thorfinn then asked permission to leave the house, but this was refused. Rognvald did let the woman and servants out, but Thorfinn and his bodyguards were left to die in the flames. Earl Thorfinn kicked out a wooden panel in the house, and carrying his wife Ingibjorg in his arms, he ran out under the cover of the smoke and darkness. He then rowed a boat over the Pentland Firth to safety in Caithness where he was hidden by his supporters. Earl Rognvald knew nothing of his uncle's escape.

Earl Rognvald now claimed all of the islands as his own and made Thorfinn's supporters swear an oath of allegiance to him. He then returned to his hall in Kirkwall and began to gather together provisions for Yule. Rognvald still needed to get malt for brewing ale for the Yule celebrations, and so he set out for Papa Stronsay. He stayed on the island that night with his men and they made a good fire to warm themselves by. It was then that Rognvald realised that his life was in danger, as the *Orkneyinga Saga* says:

> Now the earl made a slip of the tongue: he said this, "We shall be old enough before this fire is burnt out." But he meant to say that they would be warm enough before the fire was burnt out. And when he noticed his mistake, he said, "I have never made a slip of the tongue till now, so far as I remember; and it comes now to my mind that King Olaf my foster-father said at Stiklestad, when I noticed his slip of the tongue, that, if it so befell that I made a slip of the tongue, I should have but a short time to live. It may be that kinsman Thorfinn is alive."

Birsay Village from Links – Orkney Library & Archive

Earl Rognvald was right, because at that very moment Earl Thorfinn and his men had surrounded the house and built wood up against the doors and set it alight. Earl Thorfinn gave permission to all but Earl Rognvald and his men to leave the burning building. A man dressed in linen clothes came to the door and Thorfinn thought he was a deacon and ordered his men to help him out. The man put his hand on the bar across the door and vaulted over the heads of the men outside. Earl Thorfinn knew that only Earl Rognvald was capable of such a feat and ordered his men to pursue him. Thorfinn's men split up into groups to search for Rognvald; Thorkel Fosterer led the group who searched the shore. They were attracted by the barking of a dog among the rocks, and found Rognvald hiding there. He had been carrying his lapdog with him and it was this pet that betrayed his whereabouts. As nobody else would kill Earl Rognvald, Thorkel Fosterer did the slaying, because he had sworn to always do what was in the best interest of Earl Thorfinn. Earl Rognvald's body was taken to Papa Westray for burial while Earl Thorfinn sailed back to Kirkwall in Rognvald's ship. Earl Rognvald's supporters gathered on the shore to help unload the malt, but they were attacked by Earl Thorfinn and his men and killed. Earl Thorfinn spared one man in order to take the news of Earl Rognvald's death to King Magnus in Norway. This meant that Earl Thorfinn the Mighty (as he was popularly known) controlled all of Orkney and Shetland, as well as nine earldoms in Scotland, all of the Hebrides and a large realm in Ireland.

News of Earl Rognvald's death was regarded as a terrible tragedy, especially by his foster-brother, King Magnus the Good. He now ruled Norway with his uncle, King Harald Sigurdsson, better known as Harald Hard-ruler. Magnus died the following year, and was succeeded by King Harald. Earl Thorfinn wasted no time in sending messages of support to King Harald, which were received warmly. Thorfinn visited him in Norway in 1048 before heading to Rome on a pilgrimage. He returned to his hall in Birsay where he built a grand church dedicated to Christ. This was the seat of the first bishop of Orkney. Earl Thorfinn the Mighty died in his bed around the year 1065 and was buried in Christ's Kirk in Birsay. He was succeeded by his two sons, Paul and Erlend.

Heimskringla records that King Harald Hard-ruler was an oppressive sovereign, as his nickname suggests. He had persuaded Finn Arnisson to send word to his brother Kalf that if he returned to Norway he would have his estate returned to him and he would become the king's man. Kalf Arnisson returned and joined the king on a raid against the Danes. King Harald Hard-ruler split his force into two, giving the command of one of the forces to Kalf. He was to lead an attack, which would be backed by the king's force. When Kalf Arnisson landed he was attacked by a superior force and killed. King Harald's force only arrived when Kalf and his men had been cut down. The king was suspected of deliberately sending Kalf Arnisson to his death in revenge for his part in the killing of his half-brother, King Olaf the Saint. Finn Arnisson certainly thought so and left Norway to become a powerful chieftain in Denmark.

A power struggle in England in 1066 led Earl Tostig, the brother of King Harold Godwinson, to go to Norway and seek the backing of King Harald Hard-ruler in an attempt to gain the English throne. King Harald Hard-ruler had a tenuous claim to the English throne through an old agreement with the kings of Denmark. Tostig persuaded King Harald to attack England, assuring him that the English noblemen would give their support to his cause. King Harald Hard-ruler gathered a huge army that was carried in two hundred and forty warships, supported by numerous smaller supply ships. They sailed first to Shetland and then to Orkney where the king gathered more men as well as the two earls, Paul and Erlend. The king was accompanied by his son Olaf, as well as his wife Ellisif and their daughters Maria and Ingegerd. King Harald Hard-ruler's wife and daughters remained behind in Orkney while his battle fleet sailed south to attack England. After burning Scarborough and fighting against English armies, King Harald Hard-ruler arrived at York. The town surrendered on Sunday 24th September 1066 and hostages were exchanged. Later that night King Harold Godwinson arrived with his army and occupied the town. The following day King Harald Hard-ruler had breakfast on his ship and made ready to march inland to York. It was a hot day, so they left their ring-mail 'brynies' onboard their ships; this was to prove a fatal mistake. As they neared York they saw the cloud of dust raised by the advancing army. When it became apparent that they were under attack, the Norwegian army retreated to Stamford Bridge, where they had a strategic advantage over the superior English force. Three fast riders were dispatched to the Norwegian ships to bring the rest of the army to their aid. The force that remained with the ships included the king's son Olaf Haraldsson and the two Orcadian earls. They arrived too late to save King Harald Hard-ruler, who was killed by an arrow in the throat. The battle raged all day, but by evening the defeated Norsemen were offered peace terms to leave England. Olaf Haraldsson accepted, and together with the two earls sailed to Orkney. The *Orkneyinga Saga* records a tragic story, that at the very hour of King Harald Hard-ruler's death his daughter Maria fell dead in Orkney, as '*...men say that they had but one life between them'*. Olaf remained in Orkney over the winter of 1066, returning to Norway the following year. King Harold Godwinson marched his army to Hastings where he was defeated by William the Bastard of Normandy. History would later give the illegitimate Duke of Normandy the new and more respectable name of William the Conqueror. It is ironic that this Duke of Normandy was descended from Earl Rognvald of More, just the same as the earls of Orkney who had fought against King Harold Godwinson at Stamford Bridge.

An Orkney beach – Raymond Parks

BROUGH OF DEERNESS

The Brough of Deerness is a natural cliff stack with an extensive Norse archaeological site on the top.

From the air or in plan it can be seen that the chapel lies more or less at the half-way point of the stack. The southern half has a different appearance from the northern part. To the southern, or landward, side the ground is marked by many circular depressions. Although these have from time to time been interpreted as representing the remains of Celtic monastic cells, it does seem that most if not all are actually are the result of the Brough being used for target practice in the two world wars! The Well is in the centre of a larger depression.

It is thought that a narrow neck of land may have once connected to the Brough, and has subsequently fallen away. Running right along the southern edge of the Brough are the remains of what was once a substantial wall. Nowadays, having scaled the narrow path, we come to the top of the stack around the eastern end of the wall. There is, however, a break or possible entrance through the wall towards the west end – more or less opposite the part closest to the mainland. It is not known at what date this wall was built. It has been suggested that it may be much earlier than the Norse period, possibly being erected as part of the defences, during the Iron Age (*c*.BC 600 to 400AD.) Alternatively, it might have been put up as part of the process of making the stack into a monastery, enhancing the separation of the secular and holy. The foundations of a possible gate-house, just inside the entrance, could fit with either interpretation.

The chapel and its yard are the only parts of this site to have been excavated. Christopher Morris worked here during the 1970s. Although his excavations were tightly constrained, he managed to draw out a history of development of the chapel, and assembled all the available historical information. Much of the information here is derived from his report.[1] The first chapel on this site was a small, wooden, and most likely rectangular, building. This is followed by a time when the chapel site was disused – and a thin scattering of what looks like settlement debris intervenes – at which point an Anglo-Saxon coin of Eadgar (later tenth century) is deposited or dropped. This means, of course, that the stone chapel which is then built on the site must be later than the coin. How much later, exactly, is not known. The chapel was a very simple affair. Built of stone and measuring only about 5m by 3m internally, the stone chapel was constructed like others in Iceland or Greenland, with its west wall in wood. An altar was centrally placed against the east wall, and down one side was a bench. Dating on stylistic grounds is always problematic, but an eleventh century date would be acceptable. It would represent one of the first or second generation of Christian churches in Scandinavia. Hundreds of years later, and even after the chapel has fallen into ruins, the site continues to be a holy presence in the community. A sixteenth century writer, Jo Ben, describes pilgrims walking two or three times around the chapel, throwing water taken from the well, and pebbles, behind them as they went. The Brough of Birsay and St Tredwell's in Papa Westray were similar places of pilgrimage. Others such as Wasbister loch and St Mary's in Damsay are known to have been places which could be resorted to for the benefit of health. People continued to visit them, in the teeth of official disapproval, long after the Reformation.

The Brough of Deerness – Orkney Library & Archive

Brough of Deerness – Richard Welsby

From the chapel enclosure northwards lie the remains of many buildings. They seem to be laid out systematically – lined up and laid out parallel to each other. The buildings are rectangular with rounded corners. They appear to line up in two rows, with a gap or path between them, and where the buildings are not end on to the path, they are parallel to it. It appears that the buildings respect the chapel and its enclosure. This certainly encourages the thought that the chapel and the buildings may be of one period, and possibly designed for a single purpose. Several authors have thought that this might be a monastery - and compare it with the Brough of Birsay. Several of the same arguments apply. Here is a site cut off from the land. As such this is ideal territory. A rich, important and possibly contemporary Norse farmer is recorded as living in Deerness. It is arguable that he might have supported the cost of such a place. The use of a stack for a community of monks, however, is much less probable than for an isolated hermitage supported by a monastic community working good land elsewhere. The use of this site as a monastery is not supported by the fact that there were only four burials in the chapel and enclosure.

The form of most of the buildings is very like that of the earlier (ninth to tenth century) Viking buildings on the Brough of Birsay. Thus, as the Birsay houses are secular, Morris would argue that these buildings could well be secular, too.

There is a great difference, however, between the access arrangements at Birsay and Deerness Broughs. A settlement would need houses, not only for people, but for cattle and sheep. Unless the Brough was attached to the land in the Viking period, it would not be possible for the inhabitants to keep cows, because they require overwintering indoors. It is suggested, therefore, that an alternative secular use should be looked for. Perhaps it might be compared with a site in Caithness, called *Lambaborg* in *Orkneyinga Saga*[2]:

> Svein gathered his forces and went over to Lambaborg, ready to take a stand. It was a safe stronghold and they stayed put there, sixty strong, fetching in all the provisions and other things they needed. The fortress stood on a sea-cliff with a stoutly-built stone wall to landward. The cliff stretched quite a distance along the coast. They committed many a robbery in Caithness, taking the loot into their stronghold, and so became thoroughly unpopular.

In this account we can see that in times of trouble or necessity it would be possible to use a fort like this for extended, but probably intermittent, periods. It is suggested that this might well account for the archaeology seen here.

Julie Gibson

[1] Morris C.D. with N. Emery "The chapel and enclosure on the Brough of Deerness, Orkney: Survey and Excavations 1975-1977", *Proc. Soc. Antiq. Scot,* 116 pp301-74.

[2] *Orkneyinga Saga* Translated with an introduction by Hermann Palsson and Paul Edwards, Penguin books, chapter 82.

The chapel on the Brough of Deerness – Orkney Library & Archive

Interior of St Magnus Cathedral – Raymond Parks

SAINT MAGNUS

The events in this chapter take place during the period 1066–1128. Earl Thorfinn the Mighty's two sons, Paul and Erlend, ruled Orkney in peace and harmony after their father's death. This peace was to come to an end when their sons were born. Earl Paul's son Hakon was proud and greedy, while Earl Erlend's son Erling was violent and hot-headed. Erlend's other son, Magnus, was said to be a pious man, who would ultimately die a martyr's death at the hands of his cousin Hakon. Magnus was made a saint some twenty years after his death and his bones still lie in a pillar of the great red sandstone cathedral in Kirkwall that is dedicated to him. Hakon's two sons, Paul and Harald, also brought strife to Orkney. Being born to different mothers, they felt jealousy and hatred towards each other that often ended in violence. Not even the accidental killing of Harald would bring peace to the war torn islands.

The life of Saint Magnus is told in the *Orkneyinga Saga*, but we do find other pieces of information in *Heimskringla* and in the *Longer Magnus Saga*. This fuller version was compiled by a cleric called Master Robert, and included a sermon preached by Robert around the year 1136. This date coincides with Earl Rognvald Kali's coming to power after using his saintly uncle's memory as a means of obtaining support (see below).

Hymn to St Magnus, in the collection of Upsalla University Library, Sweden

Earl Thorfinn the Mighty's sons, Paul and Erlend, ruled Orkney peacefully between them. They were such close friends that they didn't divide the earldom, but ruled it equally. Earl Paul had a son, Hakon, who grew up to be a very overbearing and violent man. Earl Erlend had two sons, Erling and Magnus. Erling was overbearing like his cousin Hakon, while Magnus was good-natured and pious. Hakon thought that he should have more power and wealth than his cousins, as his grandmother was a daughter of King Magnus the Good. This led to bad feeling and violence, which in turn led to the earls Paul and Erlend falling out and dividing the islands between them. The situation did not improve, and calls were made for Hakon to leave Orkney for the sake of peace. He went to visit his kinsmen in Norway and Sweden in *c.*1093 and was treated with honour and respect.

While Hakon was in Sweden he heard of a soothsayer who could see into the future. He found the man in a forest township and asked him about his fate and if he would come into a realm that he would rule alone. The soothsayer said that he would try to find out what Hakon asked, but he would need three nights to achieve his aim. Hakon left him, returning three nights later to find out what he had learnt. The soothsayer was breathing heavily and said that it had cost him much pain to see what Hakon's future held. He said that he would indeed rule Orkney alone, as would his descendants, but that it would take longer than he would like. He also warned him that in his life he would commit a crime so great that he may never atone for it. Hakon left, happy in the knowledge that one day he would indeed be the sole earl of Orkney.

According to the *Longer Magnus Saga*, Magnus Erlendsson was not always the saint that

St Magnus Church, Egilsay – Orkney Museums and Heritage

the *Orkneyinga Saga* portrays him as. It says that during Hakon's exile overseas Magnus had fallen into bad company and developed evil ways:

> …he seemed for some winters like wicked men, and as a Viking with robbers and warriors he lived by robbery and plunder, and stood by at manslaughter along with them.

Hakon returned to Norway where King Magnus Bear-legs was now the sole ruler. Hakon knew that King Magnus was greedy for power and fame, and he urged the king to lead an army west to Orkney, hoping that he would give the earldom to Hakon. Hakon persuaded King Magnus Bare-legs that if he took the Hebrides then it would give him the opportunity to raid in Ireland and Scotland. King Magnus said that he liked the idea, but that Hakon may not like the outcome, as he would claim all of the islands for himself. Hakon now grew worried and stopped encouraging the king to act, but it was too late. King Magnus Bare-legs led an expedition west in 1098, capturing the two Orkney earls and sending them to Norway. Instead of Hakon becoming earl, King Magnus set his eight-year-old son Sigurd over the islands, aided by advisers. King Magnus Bare-legs took Hakon and his cousins Erling and Magnus with him as members of his army. Magnus Erlendsson became the king's trencher bearer and waited on the king's table.

King Magnus Bare-legs led his army through the Hebrides and put all of those islands under him. He then went south to Wales, where he met an army in the Menai Straits led by two earls, Hugh the Stout and Hugh the Proud.[10] As they prepared for battle, Magnus Erlendsson refused to fight, claiming that he had no quarrel with anyone there. King Magnus Bare-legs was angered by this defiance, saying that he should go below deck and not get in men's way, but he thought that religious conviction had little to do with his actions. Magnus took out his Psalter and chanted psalms while the battle raged around him. Hugh the Proud fought bravely, and was so clad in armour that no weapon could harm him. King Magnus Bare-legs had a bow, and he ordered another bowman to aim for the eye slits on Hugh's helmet. Both men fired an arrow at Hugh the Proud. One arrow struck the earl's nose-guard while the other went straight through his eye and killed him. The fatal shot was said to have been fired by the king.

After his victory in battle, King Magnus Bare-legs claimed all of Anglesey for himself and then returned north to Scotland. The king was very angry with Magnus Erlendsson, saying that he had behaved in an unmanly fashion in the battle. One night Magnus Erlendsson made up his bed to look as though he was lying in it then slipped unseen over the side of the king's ship and swam ashore. He was dressed only in his underclothes as he ran towards a wood for shelter. He injured his foot as he ran and was forced to climb to the top of a tree and spend the night there. In the morning King Magnus Bare-legs saw that he was absent and ordered his men to his bunk to wake him. They returned with the news that he was gone. King Magnus Bare-legs ordered the bloodhounds to be unleashed, and the king's men followed them as they ran towards the woods. One dog found the tree where Magnus Erlendsson was hiding and

---

[10] Hugh the Stout was Hugh of Avranches, Earl of Chester, while Hugh the Proud was Hugh of Montgomery, Earl of Shrewsbury.

started to run round it, barking loudly. Magnus threw a stick at the dog, which hit it on the leg and caused it to run away with its tail between its legs. Magnus was not found by the king's men, and was able to slip away to the court of the Scottish king. He later went to Wales and to England, but he never returned to Orkney so long as King Magnus Bare-legs lived.

King Magnus Bare-legs claimed all of the Scottish islands from the king of Scots, and was granted all of the islands that he could sail around in a ship with the rudder set. This would mean that the ship needed deeper water to sail in and so some of the smaller islands near to the shore couldn't be claimed. King Magnus Bare-legs tricked the king of Scots by having a small boat dragged across the isthmus of Kintyre while he sat in the stern with his hand on the tiller. In that way he claimed all of Kintyre for himself. This is a comparable story to the one found in the mythical chapters at the beginning of the *Orkneyinga Saga* when the sons of Gor claim land from the sons of Nor in the same fashion.

King Magnus Bare-legs spent the winter of 1098–99 in the Hebrides. His friend, Kali Sæbjornsson, had been badly injured in the battle of the Menai Straits and was dying. Kali advised the king to be on the lookout for deserters, because many men had already left for home without leave. The king held a roll call, and was shocked to discover how many men had already left him. Kali Sæbjornsson died soon after this. King Magnus Bare-legs gave Kali's son, Kol Kalisson, Earl Erlend's daughter Gunnhild in marriage, along with an estate in Orkney. They returned to Kol's estate at Agder in Norway where their two children were born, a son called Kali and a daughter called Ingirid. King Magnus Bare-legs returned to Orkney in the spring of 1099 where he heard that the two Orkney earls he had sent into exile in Norway had both died. Paul had died in Nidaros[11] while Erlend died in Bergen.

King Magnus Bare-legs made a second raid on Ireland, spending the winter of 1102–1103 in Connaught. Here Snorri's *Heimskringla* is at odds with the *Orkneyinga Saga*: it claims that it was this second expedition that saw Erling and Magnus Erlendsson being taken from Orkney by the king, and that Magnus had escaped from the king's clutches during this raid. The two accounts also disagree about the death of Erling Erlendsson, the brother of Magnus. The *Orkneyinga Saga* says that he died in 1098 at the battle of the Menai Straits, while *Heimskringla* has him dying with King Magnus Bare-legs in Ulster in 1103. King Magnus raided throughout Ireland and had won much land during the summer of 1103. He went ashore on 24th August, the feast day of St Bartholomew, to receive cattle that were to be slaughtered to provide food for the return journey. His army was attacked and defeated by the Irish on their way back to their ships with the cattle. *Heimskringla* paints a vivid account of how splendid King Magnus Bare-legs looked at his final battle in Ulster:

> King Magnus had his helm on his head and a red shield whereon a lion was laid in gold; he was girded with a sword called Legbiter, the best of weapons; its hilt was of walrus tooth and the handle was covered with gold. He had a spear in his hand, and over his shirt he wore a red jacket, whereon a lion was sewn with gold silk both in front and behind; it was the talk of men that no one had seen a manlier or bolder man.

---

[11] The modern day city of Trondheim.

King Magnus Bare-legs was wounded by a spear driven through both his legs, above the knees, but he broke the spear shaft and made a joke of it. He was then struck on the neck with an axe, which proved fatal. The remains of his defeated army returned to Orkney, where the king's son Sigurd was told of his father's death. Sigurd returned to Norway to rule his kingdom. Earl Hakon went to see King Sigurd in Norway to ask for the title of earl of Orkney in 1104 or 1105, which the king granted him.

In 1106, after Earl Hakon had ruled for just a short time, his cousin, Magnus Erlendsson arrived back in Orkney and claimed his inheritance. Hakon refused to give up part of Orkney, and prepared for battle. Magnus was popular with the local farmers, and had many relations in Orkney who wanted to see him return, so peace talks were held between the two cousins. Hakon agreed to share half of the earldom with Magnus if the king granted Magnus the title of earl. Magnus went east where he saw King Eystein, as his brother, King Sigurd, was on a crusade to the Holy Land at the time. King Eystein granted Magnus half of the earldom and the title of earl. Earl Magnus returned to Orkney and ruled peacefully with Earl Hakon for around ten years. Magnus was married to a woman of noble birth who came from Scotland. Nothing is known about her, but research has suggested that her name was Ingarth and that after her death she was buried in Egilsay.[12] The *Orkneyinga Saga* claims that Magnus resisted all temptations of the flesh, resorting to cold baths and prayer when temptation arose. It was also said that Magnus treated criminals harshly, but was fair in his judgements.

St Magnus' bones and box – Orkney Library & Archive

[12] Professor Bruce Dickins, Proceedings of the Orkney Antiquarian Society, Vol. XIII, 51–52.

After a while troublemakers started to stir up hatred between the earls. The *Longer Magnus Saga* claims that Earl Magnus was forced out of Orkney and spent a whole year at the court of the English King Henry I with all of his followers. Earl Hakon claimed all of Shetland, Orkney and Caithness as his own and ruled the earldom alone. Hakon was staying in Caithness when Magnus arrived with five ships full of well-armed men. Friends went between the two earls and a peace agreement was reached so that Magnus would once more have half of the earldom. There is no mention of this in the *Orkneyinga Saga*.

Two kinsmen, Sigurd and Sighvat Socks, spent much time with Earl Hakon, and once more poisoned his mind against his cousin, Earl Magnus. Things became so bad that the earls each gathered together an army and met at the 'Thing of the Orkneymen', the local parliament site, probably at Tingwall in Rendall. Once again a peaceful settlement was reached by the intervention of mutual friends and both sides departed after swearing oaths of friendship. Earl Hakon sent a message to Earl Magnus saying that they should meet for final peace talks in the island of Egilsay during Easter week the following spring. Each earl was to have two ships and a set number of men with him. Earl Magnus agreed to this, as he was keen to have peace and friendship between them.

The following Easter, Earl Magnus made ready the two ships that he was to take to the peace talks, and he picked the most peace-loving members of his followers to accompany him. As they sailed to Egilsay a huge wave rose up from out of the calm sea and broke over where Magnus sat steering the boat. He declared that this was a bad omen, and that it meant his death was close at hand. His followers urged him to turn back, but Magnus refused. After they had

St Magnus Church, Birsay – Orkney Library & Archive

arrived in Egilsay they saw that Hakon was approaching with eight ships full of well-armed warriors. Magnus knew now that Hakon meant to kill him, so he retired inland to a small church where he prayed all night. In the morning he heard mass and took the sacrament before heading to the shore where he hid with two of his men. Hakon's followers left their ships that morning and ransacked the church, but they didn't find Magnus. They then searched the island, but when Magnus saw this he shouted to them and surrendered himself. Hakon's men ran towards him, clashing their weapons against their shields and yelling. Magnus was on his knees praying when they reached him.

The *Longer Magnus Saga* differs slightly from the *Orkneyinga Saga* on this point. It says that Earl Magnus was still in the church praying when Earl Hakon's men arrived, and that Hakon ordered four of his most evil followers to go into the church and seize him. They rushed into the church with loud cries, dragging Magnus out with great violence. They bound Magnus and dragged him to where Earl Hakon stood. The point that this version is trying to make is that Hakon had violated the sanctity of the church by denying sanctuary to whoever was inside. This was a terrible sin in the medieval world, and showed how evil Earl Hakon was, since he would allow a church to be attacked.

Magnus offered Hakon three choices rather than having him killed. This was to save Hakon's soul from committing such a great sin rather than as a way of escape for Magnus. He offered to go on a pilgrimage to the Holy Land and never to return. This offer was refused. His second offer was to be imprisoned in Scotland with two companions as company and never to return to Orkney. This too was refused. Magnus's third offer was to be blinded or maimed and cast into a dungeon for the rest of his days. Hakon accepted this offer, but his chieftains refused, saying that the earldom was not to be shared and that one of the earls must die. Earl Hakon said that he was not prepared to die, so they had better kill Earl Magnus.

Ofeig, Earl Hakon's standard-bearer, was ordered to do the killing, but he refused angrily. Hakon's cook, Lifolf, was then ordered to kill Magnus. He wept bitterly, but was not in a position to refuse. Earl Magnus prayed, and then gave Lifolf his shirt, as was the custom in those days. He then said these words to Lifolf:

> "Stand thou before me, and hew on my head a great wound, for it is not seemly to behead chiefs like thieves. Take good heart, poor wretch, for I have prayed to God for thee, that He be merciful unto thee."

> After that he crossed himself, and bowed himself to the stroke; and he was struck in the middle of the head with a single blow; and so passed from the world to God.

The *Longer Magnus Saga* again differs slightly from the *Orkneyinga Saga* account:

> Lifolf hewed him on the head, then Earl Hakon said, "Hew thou a second time," and Lifolf hewed into the same wound. Magnus fell on his knees, then fell to earth.

This account suggests that Magnus was standing when he was struck on the head, which seems unlikely.

We know that Magnus was killed on 16th April; the exact year is unknown, but it is believed to have taken place during the years 1115–1117. In Master Robert's sermon, he states that Magnus died on a Monday, and that *'20 winters were passed from his martyrdom.'* As the sermon was preached in 1136 the year 1116 is implied. Whether that is the correct date or not we shall never know. Magnus was made a saint sometime around the year 1135.

Hakon refused to allow Magnus's body to be buried, then displayed a callous disregard for people's feelings by attending a feast held by Magnus's mother to celebrate the peace meeting. When only Hakon and his men arrived Thora knew that her son must be dead, but she kept silent. She waited table on Earl Hakon all night, then later when the earl was drunk she begged him to allow her to bury her son's body. *'Bury thy son where it please thee,'* said Hakon with tears in his eyes as the enormity of his crime began to dawn on him. Thora had her son's body taken to Birsay and buried in Christ Kirk.

Earl Hakon ruled for several years after that and was popular with the people, although he persecuted friends and relations of Earl Magnus. Hakon went on a pilgrimage to Rome, where the Pope absolved him of his crime, and then he travelled on to the Holy Land. He died in his bed around the year 1123, and was greatly lamented. He was succeeded by his two sons, Earl Paul the Silent and Earl Harald Smooth-tongue. Harald was the son of Hakon's mistress, Helga, the daughter of a Caithness chieftain called Moddan. There was no love lost between the two half-brothers, which led to great strife. Harald lived for some years in Caithness before he moved to Orkney with his mother, Helga, and her sister, Frakok. With him was a man called Sigurd Sham-deacon who had won fame at the court of the Scottish king. He was called Sham-deacon because he had trained as a priest. Trouble broke out almost immediately between the brothers and both sides gathered an army together. People tried to bring the two earls to terms, but Harald knew that Paul would take advice from a man called Thorkel, nicknamed the Fosterer.[13] Thorkel was a relation of St Magnus and had suffered great hardship during the persecution by Earl Hakon. Earl Harald and Sigurd Sham-deacon attacked Thorkel and killed him. Earl Paul raised a band of warriors, as did Harald, but men went between them and brought about a peaceful settlement. Sigurd Sham-deacon was banished from Orkney, along with everyone else who was considered to have had a part in the murder, and Harald paid compensation for the killing. Sigurd Sham-deacon later claimed to be King Magnus Bare-legs' son, and was involved in a civil war in Norway. He was eventually defeated and brutally tortured to death, as is recorded in *Heimskringla*.

Around the year 1128 it was decided that Earl Harald should entertain Earl Paul to a Yule feast at his estate in Orphir. As the preparations were being made, Harald's mother and her sister, Frakok, were busy sewing a beautiful linen shirt as a gift for Earl Paul. When Harald saw it he asked who this fine shirt was for. His mother said it was for his brother, and that he should not envy him this gift. Harald became jealous, and seized the shirt from them. He saw that it was as white as snow, and embroidered with gold thread. They begged him not to put it on, and Frakok

---

[13] Not to be confused with Earl Thorfinn the Mighty's foster father of the same name.

pulled off her hood and tore her hair in despair, but despite their tears Earl Harald Smooth-tongue put on the shirt. No sooner was it on his back then a great shiver ran through him, followed by burning pain. He was put to bed, but died soon after. Earl Paul now had control of all of Orkney. He guessed that the poisoned shirt was meant for him, and he had Helga and Frakok banished from the islands. They lived at Frakok's estate in Sutherland where they raised Earl Harald Smooth-tongue's son Erlend. Other children raised there were Harald's sister Margaret, Oliver the Unruly, Thorbjorn Clerk, and Erik Stay-brails. They all thought they had a claim to the earldom of Orkney, as they were related to Earl Harald Smooth-tongue, and would bring trouble to the islands in later life.

Statuette of St Magnus – Orkney Library & Archive

SHIPS

Boats are of fundamental importance to the movement of people around the coasts and islands of Europe, and out across the Atlantic. They were even more important in the early Middle Ages, before the development of networks of roads, and the Vikings were the most famous seamen of all.

It seems that sails were not used on boats in Scandinavia until shortly before the Viking Age, but once the Scandinavians had taken to the technology they showed great skill in using it. The beginning of the Viking Age seems closely related to the development of boats that were light and fast and could be sailed close to the wind. Though the Vikings are most famous for their fast fighting longships, there were many kinds of boats in use in the Norse period, from magnificently decorated royal vessels to wide high-sided cargo-carriers and small ordinary boats that were used for fishing or for daily transport.

In the twelfth century Earl Rognvald Kali and the young Earl Harald Maddadsson took passage on a merchant-ship to go to the Norwegian court. There they were inspired by travellers' tales to make an expedition to Constantinople, accompanied by young men from some of the best families. Preparations would take two years:

> It was agreed that none of them should have a ship of more than thirty thwarts for rowers except the Earl, and none should have an ornamented ship but he. Thus it would turn out that no man would envy another because one had equipped his ship or his crew better than his neighbour. John Limp-leg was to have a crusading ship built for the Earl and bestow the utmost pains on it.[1]

The Replica Gokstad Ship 'Gaia', in Kirkwall Harbour, 1991 – W Sutherland

Rivets from Scar boat burial – Orkney Library & Archive

In the meantime "King Ingi gave Earl (Rognvald) two warships, rather small, of slim lines, and specially built for rowing; and they were the fastest of ships."[2] But the lovely boats were wrecked on the coast of Shetland on the homeward journey, and a lot of cargo was lost, though all hands were saved. In Shetland Earl Rognvald went out, unrecognised, on a fishing trip in a small rowing boat with a 'penniless farmer' whose partner had not turned up, and showed his skill and strength in rowing them in and out of the dangerous current off Sumburgh Head. "Sculling" was one of the nine skills he claimed to have mastered[3].

Boats were important symbols. The kings of Norway gave gifts of longships to visiting Earls and would-be Earls, symbolising the role of the king as a source of wealth and power. Boats were also part of spiritual life, for the Vikings were like many other pagan North European peoples and buried their dead with grave-goods, which might include a boat if the family was rich or important enough.

The only archaeological evidence for Viking period boats in Orkney has been found in boat-graves in Sanday and in Rousay. Only small fragments of the wood have survived, along with the iron boat-rivets, but the positions of the fragments were all carefully recorded. The boat at Scar in Sanday was about 7.15m long, built mainly of oak, though it seems to have had a washrail of pine. There were possibly three rowlocks along the surviving side.[4] The two boat graves in the Westness cemetery in Rousay were færings, small multi-purpose boats, one 5.5m long, and the other 4.5m. The boats were "clinker-built" of oak. One had a rowlock made of antler on one side and an antler 'vadbein' for the fishing line on the other side[5]. There must have been hundreds of boats in Orkney in Viking times, but these small glimpses are all that remain.

Anne Brundle

[1] Taylor 1938, 276, ch 85

[2] Taylor 1938, 276, ch 85

[3] Taylor 1938, 279, ch 85. For Earl Rognvald's boast of his skills, Taylor 1938, 225, ch 85

[4] Owen and Dalland 1999, 39-51

[5] Kaland 1993, 315-6

Detail of ship on stone from Lärbro, Goltland

St Rognvald's Chapel, St Magnus Cathedral, Kirkwall – Orkney Library & Archive

Detail of north triforium, St Magnus Cathedral, Kirkwall – Raymond Parks

THE MIRACLES OF ST MAGNUS

The events in this chapter take place during the period c1116– 1135. The cult of St Magnus had popular support, especially in Shetland, but was suppressed by both Earl Paul and Bishop William. Earl Paul's own father had ordered the killing of Magnus, while Bishop William had been opposed by Magnus when he was earl. In order to gain the support of the church it seems that land and the cathedral church of St Magnus were promised to Bishop William, who had Magnus made into a saint. This paved the way for St Magnus's nephew to claim a share of the earldom.

Earl Paul the Silent now ruled Orkney alone, and proved to be a popular leader. Since the death of St Magnus it had been said that miracles had taken place at his tomb in Birsay. Mysterious lights were seen over the tomb and the smell of perfume hung in the air. Bishop William paid no attention to these claims, saying that it was heresy to believe such things. As Magnus had taken a rival bishop to Orkney when he was earl, threatening Bishop William's position of power in the islands, it is hardly surprising that he felt no sympathy towards Magnus. Earl Paul was angered by the claims, as Magnus had been murdered on the orders of his father. This did not stop people from visiting the tomb and claiming that they had been cured of various diseases. There is a list of miracles given in the *Orkneyinga Saga*, but they are very much the same as miracle lists of other European saints. Cures for infirmities, blindness and insanity are common claims, but there is one unusual miracle that can be traced to a European tradition.

It is said in the *Orkneyinga Saga* that there was a man in England who had lost a large amount of money by gambling with dice. He bet his ship and everything that he owned against what he had already lost. His opponent threw the dice and got two sixes. The man prayed to St Magnus that if he would save him he would give money to his shrine, and then he threw his dice. The one die turned up a six, while the other broke into two and gave him a six and a one, making a total of thirteen. He won his bet and he made a large donation of money to St Magnus's shrine. This same miracle is also said to have happened for St Olaf when he was king of Norway. *Heimskringla* tells the story of how King Olaf of Norway was in dispute with King Olaf of Sweden over territory that lay between their two countries:

> …there was a district in Hising which sometimes had gone with Norway, sometimes with Gautland. Then the kings said to each other that they would cast lots with dice for that possession; he who threw the highest number was to have it. Then the Swedish king threw two sixes and said that King Olaf had now no need to throw. The latter said whilst he shook the dice in his hands: "There are still two sixes on the dice and for the Lord my God it is an easy thing to let them turn up." He threw and two sixes came up. Then Olaf the Swedish king threw and again two sixes turned up. Thereupon Olaf, King of Norway, threw and there was a six on one dice but the other broke in bits and it became seven. He won the district.

This story is also found in medieval Spanish folk tradition, where a saint throws dice with a gambler for his soul and wins after the dice splits in two. There is also a tradition of St Bernard winning the soul of a gambler by beating him at dice.[14]

The list of miracles given in the *Orkneyinga Saga* is also found in the *Longer Magnus Saga*, but with one notable exception. The last miracle in the *Longer Magnus Saga* is colourful to say the least. Two brothers in Norway were accused of trying to cheat a powerful family, and they were seized and taken to a wood where the one considered mostly to blame was killed. His brother had his arms and legs broken, his eyes put out and his tongue cut out. A pack of wolves ran from the woods and devoured his brother's body before running back among the trees. As the injured brother lay there, more dead than alive, his thoughts turned to God and St Magnus. He was unable to pray, but he beseeched God and St Magnus in his thoughts to have mercy on him. He then became aware of a man standing over him. The man laid his hands on the injured man's arms and legs and they were healed. He then laid his hands on the stump of the injured man's tongue, and it became whole again, as did his eyes when they were touched. The man said:

> What is thy name most noble lord?

to which the stranger replied:

> Here is earl Magnus, but mind well to keep what thou has vowed to God.

The man then begged St Magnus to bring his brother back to life. Suddenly, the wolves ran out of the wood and back to the remains of the dead body where they vomited up all of the flesh and bone that they had eaten. St Magnus raised his right hand over the remains and said a blessing and the body became whole again. Then he said another blessing and the dead man rose up alive.

It is interesting to note that the majority of the miraculous cures recorded in the *Orkneyinga Saga* are claimed by people from Shetland, an area that was sympathetic to Magnus. A large number of these miracles happened to a Shetland farmer called Bergfinn Skatisson, his family and servants. Magnus had ruled the East Mainland and the North Isles of Orkney, and this must have extended to Shetland as well. When Magnus's nephew, Kali Kolsson (later named Rognvald Kali), claimed half of the earldom he would get most of his support from the areas that his uncle had formerly ruled, especially Shetland.

Bishop William was hostile to the cult of St Magnus and did nothing to encourage it. One summer he sailed to Norway, but was delayed in his return. Stranded in Shetland due to bad weather he was urged by a member of the ship's crew to make a vow that he would not speak against the sanctity of Magnus if the wind was to moderate so that they could sail. The bishop agreed, and the wind immediately died down, enabling them to return to Orkney. Bishop William did not honour his vow and did nothing to promote Magnus as a saint. The *Orkneyinga Saga* claims that the bishop went blind in Christ Kirk, but regained his sight after praying at St Magnus's tomb. He then had the bones of Magnus exhumed and tested a knuckle

---

[14] I am indebted to Professor Bo Almqvist for his help in providing information on this folk tradition.

bone in holy fire, but it did not burn. The *Orkneyinga Saga* claims that it took on a golden glow, and even turned into the shape of a cross. The *Longer Magnus Saga* claims that the bone shone like gold and turned into a cross when shown to the Pope.

St Magnus appeared in a dream to a farmer from Westray called Gunni and ordered him to tell the bishop that he wanted his bones to be moved from Birsay to Kirkwall. Gunni was afraid of what Earl Paul would say, so he stayed at home. The following night Magnus appeared to him again, only this time he was angry. He ordered Gunni to go to Birsay with his message, and warned him that he would be punished in this world and the next if he didn't. Gunni went to Birsay and told his dream to Bishop William in Christ Kirk in front of the congregation, which included Earl Paul. The *Orkneyinga Saga* says:

> Earl Paul kept silence as if he had water in his mouth, and turned red as blood.

Despite the hostility of Earl Paul to the cult of St Magnus, Bishop William had Magnus's grave opened. They found to their amazement that his bones had nearly risen to the surface. The bones of St Magnus were taken to Kirkwall where they were enshrined in St Olaf's Kirk. Ultimately St Magnus Cathedral would be built as a shrine to house his relics.

Carvings of Rognvald, Kol and Bishop William in St Rognvald's Chapel, St Magnus Cathedral, Kirkwall
– Orkney Library & Archive

KIRKWALL

Although there were people living in Kirkwall before the Vikings (the remains of an Iron Age broch lie under the Royal Bank at the head of Victoria Street) Kirkwall itself came into existence in Norse times. The name Kirkwall comes from Old Norse meaning church-bay. At the time of the sagas, the town was an entirely different shape. The curving present-day main street of Bridge Street / Albert Street / Broad Street marks what were the edges of the bay. In fact, at some point during Norse times, a wharf for cargo boats was cut back into the rock of the shore in front of the Cathedral. This whole bay has since been infilled and built upon, over many generations, until now only the "Peedie Sea" boating lake is left of the original inlet.

Door of St Olaf's Kirk (not in original location), Kirkwall – Orkney Museums and Heritage

It is often said of Kirkwall that it is "Norway's best preserved medieval town." The original layout of the plots, with houses and shops standing gable ends onto the harbour, and ginnels or alleys running between some of the plots to a back road, is in a very traditional Norse style. The first church in Kirkwall was situated on Albert Street, near the alley called St Olaf's Wynd. An arch, now moved and rebuilt as a garden gate, is all that remains above ground of the church. Burials are commonly disturbed in the vicinity, however, and mark land formerly set aside as a churchyard. Kirkwall was a busy town in the time of the Sagas. For instance, *Orkneyinga Saga* relates the story of Earl Thorfinn surprising and murdering thirty of Earl Rognvald's supporters, who were amongst a crowd who came, mistakenly, to meet his boat from Papa Stronsay (where Earl Rognvald had been killed). The Saga also relates a story of a murder in an ale-house occurring in the twelfth century, thus giving Kirkwall the distinction of having the first recorded pub in Scotland. By observing the buried soils beneath Albert Street, at times when pipes are being dug up, archaeologists have discovered evidence for leather-working, metal working, and butchery. Some of the soils are waterlogged, providing conditions which will potentially preserve a huge range of materials, so perhaps even boats may yet be found. It is entirely possible that Kirkwall has archaeological remains as important as those of York and Dublin - towns which were founded by Vikings at about the same time.

In 1136, at the other end of the modern street, a then "greenfield" site on the edge of town was identified for the building of the Cathedral in Kirkwall. The founder of the cathedral, Earl Rognvald, commissioned it to house St Magnus' relics in unrivalled magnificence, thus securing the allegiance of the population and the spiritual help of St Magnus, his uncle, for his fight against his rival Earl Paul. At a time when God and his saints were truly a force to be reckoned with, Rognvald's future possession of the Earldom would rely on support both temporal and spiritual. Like the town itself, the Cathedral started much smaller, and has expanded out from its centre. In its initial phase it was probably more or less symmetrical about the crossing, and would have extended for some three bays (count the windows) to the east and west of the transepts. St Magnus' remains were probably originally housed in a highly decorated and gilded shrine displayed over the altar, possibly in an apse.

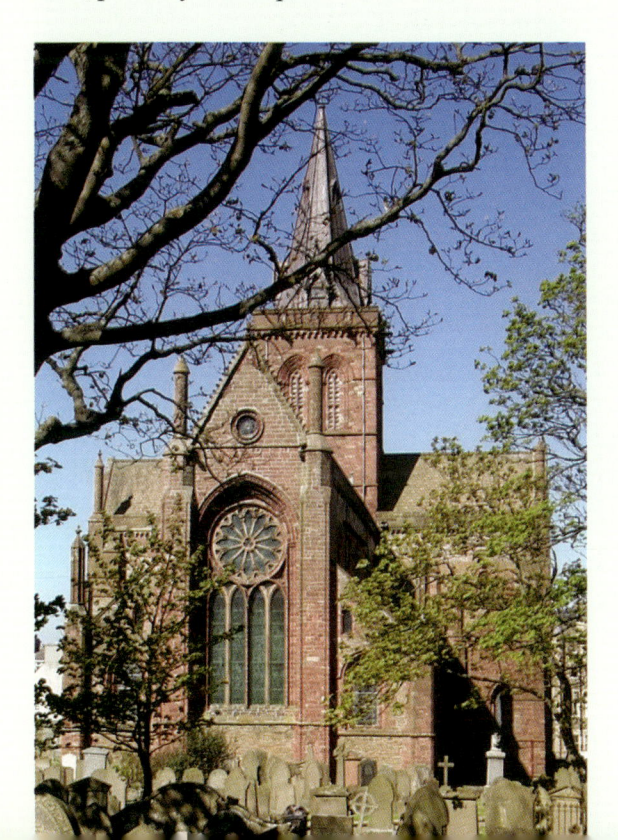

The bright red and white stone of the cathedral, built in the Norman fashion for Romanesque architecture, was beautifully worked by masons who had been involved in building Durham Cathedral. This style places Orkney at the height of European fashion at the time. This should not come as a surprise, in light of the fact that by going on a crusade Earl Rognvald was doing what would have been very much *de rigueur* for Christian princes and nobility. In the centuries which followed the translation of the miraculous relics of St Magnus to the cathedral, it became a focus of pilgrimage, and no doubt a great source of visitor income, helping to secure the fortunes of the town itself. St Magnus Cathedral is now owned by the people of Orkney, and managed by the local authority.

Julie Gibson

St Magnus Cathedral, Kirkwall
– Photographs by Raymond Parks

The Lady Stone, St Mary's Kirk, Burwick, showing carving
believed to be footprints left by St Magnus – Keith Allardyce

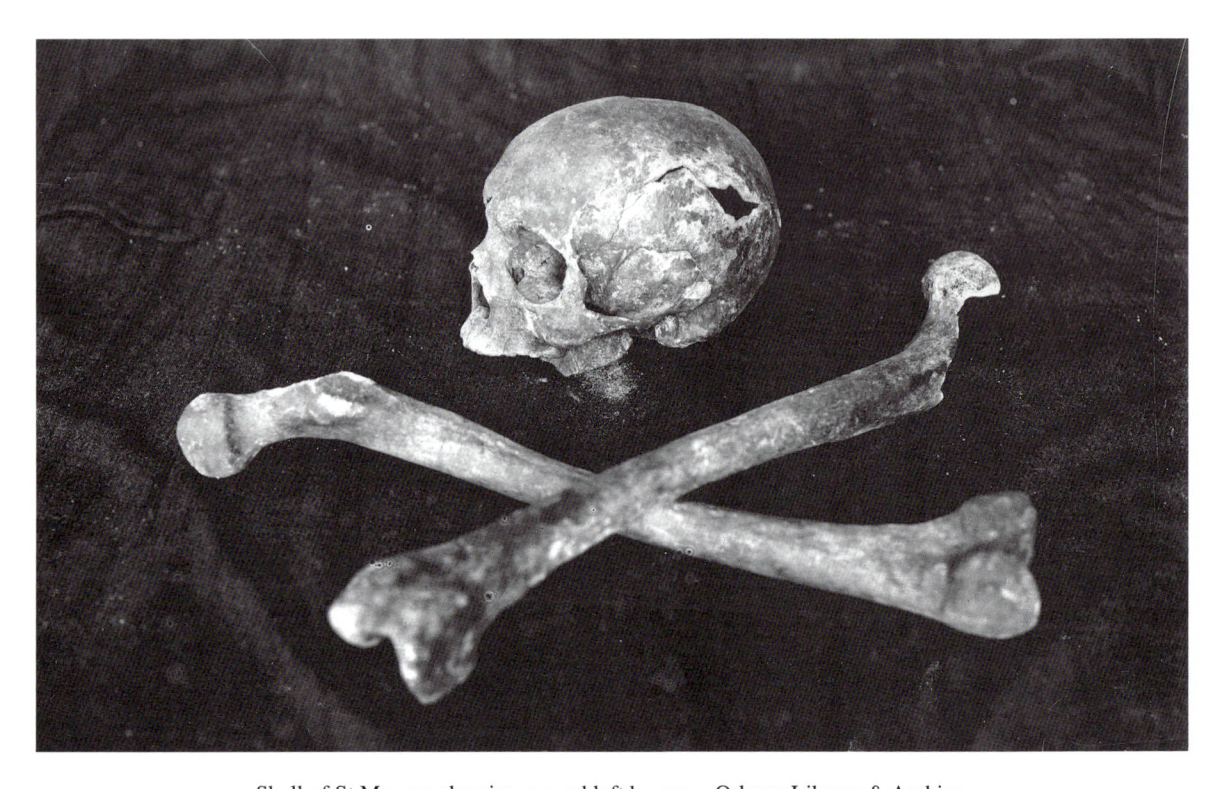

Skull of St Magnus showing wound left by axe – Orkney Library & Archive

ROGNVALD KALI BECOMES EARL

The events in this chapter take place during the period 1129–1136. When St Magnus's nephew, Rognvald Kali, claimed a half-share of the earldom of Orkney, Earl Paul refused. Rognvald was forced to enlist the help of Earl Paul's enemies with promises of a share of the earldom. His efforts failed until he made a vow to build a cathedral in honour of his kinsman, St Magnus. His claim had the backing of most of Shetland, but the Orkneymen stood by Earl Paul. Rognvald only gained the earldom as a result of the intervention of a renegade warrior called Svein Asleifsson. During the twelfth century, we start to see the rise of the chieftains, warrior landowners who were in command of their own band of fighting men. Svein Asleifsson would become the most powerful of all these chieftains, rivalling even the power of the earl.

The story of Earl Rognvald Kali is told in the *Orkneyinga Saga*. In Norway St Magnus's nephew Kali Kolsson had grown up to be a promising man of medium height and with light chestnut hair. He was a poet and claimed to be a master of board games, sports, runes, skiing, shooting, rowing and playing the harp. In the year 1129, King Sigurd, called the Crusader because of the pilgrimage he had made to the holy land, was king of Norway. Kali Kolsson went to see the king and was granted half of the earldom of Orkney and given the title of earl. King Sigurd also gave him a new name, Rognvald, as he said that Earl Rognvald Brusisson was the most accomplished of all the earls of Orkney, and the name would bring him luck. A change of king after Sigurd's death in 1130 saw Rognvald Kali out of favour, as he had backed a rival claimant. When this rival king, Harald Gilli, finally gained control of Norway, Rognvald Kali was once more granted the title of earl. Envoys were sent to Earl Paul in 1134 claiming half of the earldom, but he refused to share power. The envoys then went south to Sutherland to visit Frakok and offer her a share of the earldom for her grandson, Oliver the Unruly, if she raised an army to fight Earl Paul. Oliver the Unruly was the son of Thorljot of Rackwick and Frakok's daughter Steinvor, but he had no right to claim a share of the earldom of Orkney. Frakok was eager to gain power in Orkney and agreed to raise a force and sail there the following midsummer.

Rognvald Kali sailed to Shetland with five or six ships and lay at anchor in Yell Sound. He still had heard nothing from Frakok regarding her army. Earl Paul was attending a feast held by Sigurd of Westness in Rousay when the news reached him that Rognvald had landed in Shetland. He was also told that Frakok and Oliver the Unruly had raised a force against him and that he now had to face two enemies. Earl Paul sought the advice of his closest friends, but he eventually decided to raise an army in Orkney to fight in defence of his realm. Paul intended to sail to Shetland to attack Rognvald's force, but was told that twelve ships had been sighted sailing through the Pentland Firth. Earl Paul turned his ships to meet these vessels, lashing his ships together off the eastern coast of Tankerness. Oliver's ships sailed in past the

Mull Head of Deerness and towards Paul's fleet. A violent battle ensued, but Oliver's ships were small and poorly manned and were cleared by Paul's men. Oliver the Unruly attacked the earl's ship, jumping on board and throwing a spear at Earl Paul. The spear struck him on the shield and knocked him over, but his bodyguard, Sven Breast-rope, threw a rock at Oliver that struck him on the chest and knocked him overboard. His men pulled Oliver out of the water, but he was unconscious and they didn't know if he was dead or alive. Without their leader Oliver's men cut the ropes holding the ships together and fled the scene of the battle. When Oliver recovered his senses he tried to get them to return to the fight, but to no avail. Earl Paul chased the remaining ships out of Orkney waters and then returned to claim five ships that had belonged to Oliver and were now abandoned.

After his victory against Oliver, Earl Paul sailed to Shetland and came on Rognvald's ships unawares. Rognvald was on land and the ships were lightly guarded; his men were soon killed and the ships captured. Rognvald and his men ran to the shore and challenged Earl Paul to come ashore and fight, but Paul told him to get ships and fight him at sea. With that, Earl Paul took Rognvald's ships and headed south to Orkney. Rognvald had to take passage on a merchant ship to return to Norway. He gained little credit from this loss, and his expedition was treated with derision. Earl Paul ordered that a chain of beacons be set up on Fair Isle and throughout Orkney. They would be lit as a warning if Rognvald and his men were seen sailing from Shetland.

That winter Earl Paul held a great Yule feast at his estate in Orphir where he entertained his most powerful chieftains. One unexpected visitor was a young man called Svein, the son of Olaf Hrolfsson whom Earl Paul had put in charge of his lands at Duncansby in Caithness. Svein came with the news that his own father had been killed by Oliver the Unruly, who had burnt him to death in his house, along with six other men. Olaf had brought a ship to Earl Paul's force the previous summer when they defeated Oliver off Tankerness. Earl Paul gave Svein a good seat in his hall, and invited him to join the feast. News was later brought to Earl Paul that Svein's brother Valthjof had been drowned while sailing from Stronsay to attend the earl's feast. He decided to withhold this news from Svein, as he had enough to worry about.

Svein, who was later called Asleifsson after his mother, was seated opposite Svein Breast-rope. There was a bitter rivalry between them, and soon Svein Breast-rope started to complain that Svein Asleifsson had a smaller drinking horn and wasn't playing fair with the drinking. Drinking contests were popular at feasts, but they were highly regulated to ensure fairness between the drinkers. This bad feeling resulted in Svein Breast-rope muttering:

> *Svein must be the death of Svein, and Svein shall be Svein's death.*

When the earl rose to go to hear mass Svein Asleifsson followed him to the church. He was stopped by Eyvind, a well-respected warrior who had been acting as cup-bearer to the two Sveins. He asked Svein Asleifsson if he had heard what the other Svein has said about killing him. Svein Asleifsson said that he had not. Eyvind gave Svein an axe and told him to hide behind a large flagstone that formed part of the ale store and get ready to strike first. If Svein Breast-rope's kinsman Jon was walking in front of him then Svein Asleifsson was to strike him from the front, but if Jon was behind he was to strike from the back. Svein Asleifsson waited until his enemy approached. Jon was in the lead, so he waited until he passed and then struck Svein Breast-rope on the forehead with the axe. The mortally wounded Svein saw the figure of a man in the doorway in front of him, and he drew his sword and split the man's head in two. Svein Breast-rope had no idea that this was his kinsman Jon that he had just killed. He fell to the floor and died later that night. Svein Asleifsson made good his escape and rode a horse over the Orphir hills to the Bay of Firth, and then took a boat to the small island of Damsay. Here he stayed until he was taken in by Bishop William who lived on Egilsay. The bishop was pleased that Svein Breast-rope had been killed as he still practiced the old pagan religion.

When Earl Paul's men found the body of Jon and the unconscious Svein, the earl ordered everyone to their seats to see who was missing. When they saw that Svein Asleifsson's seat was empty they knew that he must have attacked Svein Breast-rope, but Earl Paul said that he must have had a reason for the killing. He said that if Svein surrendered himself into the earl's power and explained his actions, then he should be pardoned, but if he stayed away he would be made an outlaw. Svein sailed to the Hebrides and after a while Earl Paul declared him an outlaw. Svein Asleifsson would return and rise to power: the maker and breaker of earls.

Orphir Hill – Steve Callaghan

Rognvald Kali Kolsson had not abandoned his hopes of becoming the earl of Orkney and Shetland. He gathered a force together, and by March 1136 they lay off the Hen Islands in Norway before sailing west. News came to Rognvald of the beacons that Earl Paul had built, and that the people of Orkney would rise up against him if he was to attack. Rognvald's father, Kol Kalisson, was a wise man. He advised Rognvald that he should put his faith in God and in holy St Magnus, who was his uncle. He said that Rognvald should make a vow that if he gained the earldom of Orkney then he would build a great stone church in Kirkwall dedicated to St Magnus. The relics of Magnus would rest in the church, and it would be the seat of the bishop of Orkney. Rognvald agreed, and the vow was made. Historians point to this as the real reason why Bishop William suddenly changed his position on the sanctity of Magnus after an unexplained trip to Norway. The cathedral church of St Magnus certainly brought a great deal more power and wealth to Bishop William and the church in general.[15]

Rognvald's ships headed west to Shetland, where they received a warm welcome. Kol's thoughts turned to the Fair Isle beacon, and how it could be put out of action. If this beacon was lit then it would alert Earl Paul's men in Orkney and Rognvald would have no hope of defeating the army that would be raised against him. Kol had staying with him an old man called Uni who was considered a wise and cunning man. Kol asked Uni to devise a plan to sabotage the Fair Isle beacon. Uni said that he would consider the question and return with an answer. Kol was also a cunning man, and he decided on a plan to trick Dagfinn, the keeper of the Fair Isle beacon. He sailed south with some ships, stopping when he thought that they would be visible from Fair Isle. He then had the sails hoisted to half-mast, but ordered the

The isle of Damsay (beyond the Holm of Grimbister) – Steve Callaghan

[15] Thomson, William P.L., *The New History of Orkney*. Mercat Press, Edinburgh. 2001. 104–106.

men to row backwards so that the ships remained fairly stationary in the water. He then slowly hoisted the sails so that it looked as if the ships were getting closer. Dagfinn saw this and lit the Fair Isle beacon. Soon the beacon on North Ronaldsay was ablaze, and from the hilltops of Orkney the beacons burned. Earl Paul gathered his warriors ready for battle, expecting Rognvald to attack at any time, but he never came. Kol turned his ships back to Shetland; his plan had worked.

Dagfinn sailed south from Fair Isle to join Earl Paul's force. When it seemed obvious that it had been a false alarm the men started to quarrel, saying that Dagfinn must have seen some fishing boats. Dagfinn tried to blame Thorstein Ragnasson of North Ronaldsay for lighting his beacon first. Thorstein said that he lit his beacon when he saw the Fair Isle one ablaze, and the two men argued until Thorstein struck Dagfinn on the head with his axe, killing him instantly. Fighting broke out between Earl Paul's supporters, and it was only with the greatest of difficulty that the earl managed to separate them.

Kol returned to Shetland and said to Uni that it was now his turn to do something to put the Fair Isle beacon out of action. Uni took three young Shetland men with him and they sailed to Fair Isle in a six-oared fishing boat. Uni claimed to be a Norwegian who was married in Shetland, and that the young men were his sons. He said that they had been attacked by Rognvald's men and robbed of everything that they had. The boys returned home, saying that they were going back to the fishing. Uni remained on Fair Isle, and gained the trust of Erik, the man who was now in charge of the beacon. Uni offered to watch the beacon by day, as he had nothing else better to do, to which Erik readily agreed. Uni now carried water to the beacon and soaked all of the wood that was piled there. Rognvald had picked a spring tide accompanied by an easterly wind to sail from Shetland to Westray, as he knew that the wind would be against Earl Paul's ships sailing from the Mainland to Westray. When Erik saw the sails appear on the horizon he hurriedly prepared to sail to the earl in Orkney, and sent word to Uni to light the beacon. When the messenger arrived at the beacon Uni was gone, and the wood was so wet that it wouldn't burn. Erik then guessed what had happened, and sailed south to warn Earl Paul.

Rognvald's ships sailed unhindered to Westray where they landed at Pierowall. The islanders rose against him, but two Westray chieftains, Kugi and Helgi, had a meeting with the Westray men and urged them to come to terms. They submitted themselves to Rognvald and swore oaths of loyalty to him. Earl Paul held a meeting on the Mainland to ask his advisers what should be done. Some urged him to make peace with Rognvald and share the earldom, while others urged him to fight. Some thought that Rognvald could be paid off with money. Rognvald sent a messenger to Bishop William and asked that he should mediate between them. A truce was granted for two weeks while a settlement was attempted.

Svein Asleifsson had left the Hebrides in the spring of 1136 and was staying with Earl Maddad in Athol. He was married to Margaret, the daughter of Earl Hakon and the half-sister of Earl Paul. She had been raised by her aunt Frakok in Sutherland and shared her grandmother's greed for power. Svein had heard of the power struggle in Orkney and decided to return home.

He also stayed with Frakok's brother, Earl Ottar, in Thurso and promised to try to claim half of the earldom for Erlend, the son of Earl Harald Smooth-tongue, who had died when he put on the poisoned shirt.

Earl Paul was staying with Sigurd of Westness in Rousay during the truce, and he had gone to hunt otters among the rocks by the sea on the west coast of the island. Svein Asleifsson had arrived in a merchant ship, so as not to draw attention to himself. He saw the earl's men by the shore on Rousay, so he ordered that most of his men should hide under their sleeping bags while the others spoke to the earl's men. On hearing that Earl Paul was there they sailed their ship around a headland, then put ashore and attacked the earl's men. The earl's men were killed, and Earl Paul was captured and taken away to his half-sister Margaret in Athol. She seems to have had a simpler and more brutal way of dealing with him than her grandmother had tried when she made him a poisoned shirt to wear. It is said in the *Orkneyinga Saga* that Earl Paul gave up his earldom willingly, but the rumour soon got out that Svein had blinded him and had him cast into a dungeon, and that Margaret had paid a man to murder him. Her reason for doing this was to open the way for her son, Harald Maddadsson, to claim a share of the Orkney earldom.

When Earl Paul didn't return, a search party was sent out and they found the bodies of his men, as well as the bodies of some strangers. The earl was nowhere to be seen. Without a leader the chieftains went to Rognvald and swore oaths of loyalty to him. He held a meeting in Kirkwall that was attended by the leading men of the islands who swore oaths to him. During this meeting Svein Asleifsson arrived and went to see Bishop William. He told him of Earl Paul's kidnapping, and that the earl would never return. News of this was brought to Rognvald, and when the chieftains heard the news they all swore oaths of loyalty to Earl Rognvald.

Interior of St Magnus Cathedral, Kirkwall – Raymond Parks

EARL ROGNVALD'S PILGRIMAGE

Earl Rognvald's pilgrimage to the Holy Land and journey through the Mediterranean, returning by way of Constantinople and Rome, is a dramatic record of international contact and participation in the medieval world-scene. Rognvald was not the first earl to go so far east, but we know far more about his journey than Hakon Paulsson's, because of the lengthy saga account, based around stanzas of Rognvald's own poetry. The exuberance of this poetry gives us the spirit of adventure which seems to have been the motivating factor behind the journey. There was probably also an element of peer emulation of the famous pilgrimage undertaken in 1108 by King Sigurd Magnusson, whom Rognvald met in 1129 when he received a grant of half the Orkney earldom from him. The account of King Sigurd's pilgrimage presents it as a prestigious achievement and stresses the secular episodes, echoed in the saga account of Rognvald's deeds. More space is devoted to events in Constantinople than in Jerusalem, because the relationship with the Byzantine emperor is an important criterion in the establishing of prestige.

By 1151 the political situation in the earldom was favourable, and the Cathedral dedicated to St. Magnus was well advanced, but the Second Crusade was over. Some of the conquered lands in Syria had been lost, and although Jerusalem was still held, there was intrigue and faction in the Court of the Frankish kingdom of Jerusalem. The saga account gives no indication of any crusader intention or any military activity on behalf of the king of Jerusalem; the only incident involving action against Muslims was the capture of a Saracen merchant ship. Their fleet consisted of fifteen large ships, captained by Norwegians and Orcadians – of whom Bishop William was one, invited to join especially as interpreter.

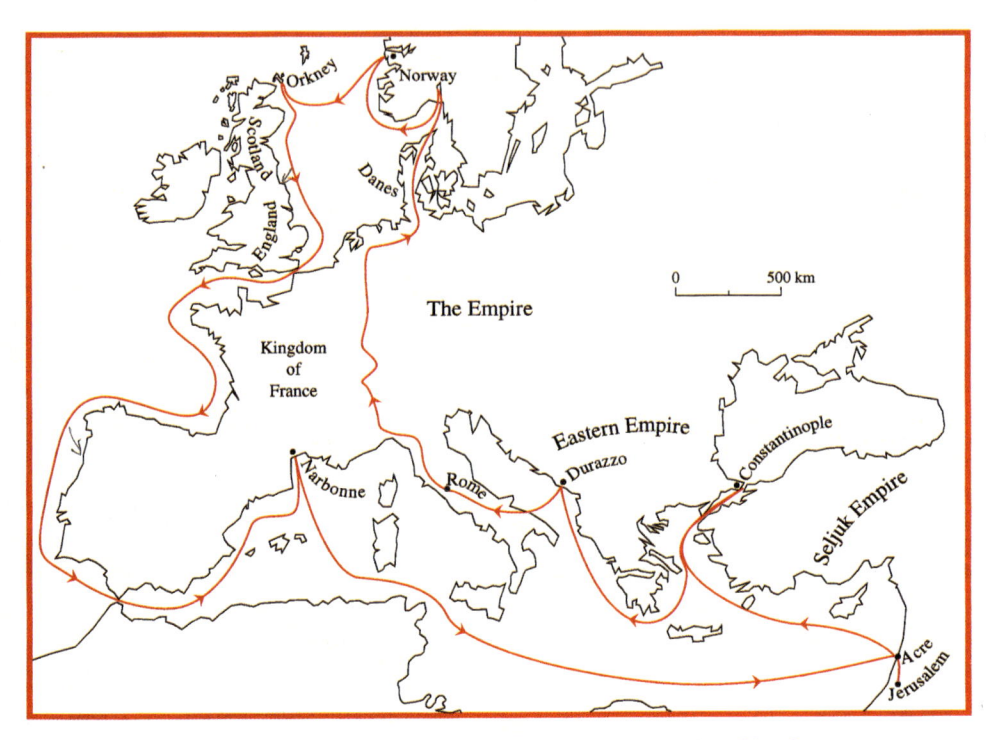

Earl Rognvald's Pilgrimage to the Holy Land 1151 - 3

Map of Earl Rognvald's route to and from the Holy Land – B E Crawford

The powerful Erling *Skakke* was another, and in the Icelandic Annals the pilgrimage is referred to as Rognvald's and Erling's.

Rognvald sailed the western route round the Iberian peninsula through the Straits of Gibraltar, having captured a castle in Galicia, then stopping off in Provence where he dallied with the lovely Lady Ermingard at Narbonne, composing many verses. These verses are influenced by courtly love motifs, and are in fact the earliest safely dateable examples of such motifs in Norse poetry. This aspect of troubadour poetry must have been picked up by Rognvald in Provence, giving us a very nice illustration of just how such cultural influences passed from the Mediterranean to the Nordic world.

After the encounter with the Saracen 'dromond'(merchant ship) the company reached the Holy Land at Acre, where disease broke out among his men and Thorbjorn the Black died (one of the four poets who were in the earl's retinue). They are then said to have visited all the most sacred places, although no details are given, except for swimming across the River Jordan (which is remarkably similar to the earlier account of King Sigurd's exploit). We can only assume that the Church of the Holy Sepulchre was visited. Far more important to the saga-writer was the visit to Constantinople, when they sailed up the Hellespont 'with great pomp,' and again 'as they knew Sigurd *Jórsalafari* ("Jerusalemfarer") had done.' They were well-received by the Emperor Manuel, who is said to have given them a great deal of money and 'offered to hire them as mercenaries if they would agree to stay on.' This is very likely to be a reference to negotiations over

View of the Temple Mount, Jerusalem – B E Crawford

whether the ship's company would join the imperial Varangian Guard, which was traditionally made up of young Scandinavian and Anglo-Saxon noble warriors. One way of financing the return journey north was to sell your ship, with its company of warriors, for service in the imperial palace guard. It is possible that the runic inscription which can still be seen on the balustrade of the balcony in Ayia Sophia is a poignant memorial to just such a young Nordic visitor, who did join the Emperor's bodyguard and carved his name - Halfdan.

However Rognvald and his company sailed west to Italy before they disembarked (presumably selling the ships off there - it is said that he had no ships when he got back to Norway), and rode to Rome before moving north over the Alps and via Denmark back to Norway. The saga account may be all about the enhancement of prestige, but that does not detract from the achievement of the earl in travelling the known world, along with his bishop. The two leaders of Orkney society set an example of devoutness; but it was the achievement of fame which was remembered and which the saga-writer comments on: 'This was a famous journey and everyone was considered the greater who had done it'(*ok varð þessi ferð in frægsta, ok þóttu þeir allir miklu meira háttar menn síðan, en aðr, er farit hofðu*).

Barbara E Crawford

Interior of Ayia Sophia, Constantinople (Istanbul) – B E Crawford

THE ADVENTURES OF EARL ROGNVALD

The events in this chapter occur during the period 1137–1153. Earl Rognvald agreed to share the earldom with Earl Paul's nephew, Harald Maddadsson. On a trip to Norway Earl Rognvald is persuaded to lead a pilgrimage to the Holy Land. This was not just a spiritual journey, but a way to gain wealth and an honourable reputation. Earl Rognvald woos a beautiful queen, captures a castle and attacks a huge ship before arriving at his destination.

Now that Rognvald was earl, he began work on building the cathedral that was to be dedicated to his uncle, St Magnus. The work began in 1137 and was overseen by Earl Rognvald's father, Kol Kalisson, and for the first three years it progressed with great speed. Money started to run out and further taxation was considered, but they knew that this would be highly unpopular. Kol suggested that the farmers should buy back their odal rights, which Earl Torf Einar had claimed after he paid the fine levied on Orkney for the killing of King Harald Fair-hair's son. The Orkneymen agreed to the deal, and got back their land rights. There was now plenty of extra money to continue the building of the cathedral. This explanation of how the money was raised is strange, as Earl Sigurd the Stout had already returned the odal rights to the Orkneymen around the year 995 in return for their support in battle.

Statuette of Rognvald, from Bishop Reid's Tower, Kirkwall – Raymond Parks

After Rognvald had been earl for two years, he was visited by Bishop Jon of Athol, who was described as looking like *'rather a strange fellow'* with a long beard that was shaved in the middle. The bishop said that Svein Asleifsson had arranged that Earl Maddad of Athol's son Harald should have a half-share of the earldom. Harald Maddadsson was only a child, but it was agreed that they would both share the earldom, but that Rognvald would be in control of the islands. This was agreed, and Earl Harald Maddadsson came to Orkney where he was fostered by Thorbjorn Clerk, the grandson of Frakok. Thorbjorn became great friends with Earl Rognvald, and he married Svein Asleifsson's sister, Ingigerd.

Svein now lived in great style in the island of Gairsay where he had a large drinking hall. He also held lands in Caithness and went raiding twice a year. Svein now wanted to have his revenge on Frakok and Oliver the Unruly for the killing of his father. He asked Earl Rognvald for support in the expedition, but he was told that Frakok and her grandson were no longer a threat to anyone. Svein reminded the earl of how he had secured the earldom for him, and said that as long as Frakok lived she would be a thorn in his side. Earl Rognvald gave him two fully-manned ships and Svein sailed to the Moray Firth to attack Frakok's house at Helmsdale in Sutherland. Oliver the Unruly had spies posted on the roads leading from Orkney, but he didn't expect an attack from the south. Svein and his men arrived at Frakok's house before Oliver was aware of them. Oliver had sixty men with him, and they fought a short battle before being driven back. Many were killed, but Oliver the Unruly escaped west over the mountains

Rognvald was (self-claimed!) an expert on the 'harp' – a literal translation – now believed to be the lyre as pictured

and fled to the Hebrides, never to be heard of again. Svein's men set fire to Frakok's house, and she died there among the flames. Svein then plundered Sutherland, and around the coast of Scotland and the Hebrides.

Thorbjorn Clerk put to death two of Svein's men who were at Frakok's burning. Earl Rognvald tried to bring peace between Svein and Thorbjorn, but the cracks were beginning to show. Both men captained ships on a raid against the Hebrides, but it ended in bitterness when Svein claimed a larger share of the plunder, leaving Thorbjorn with a small amount of the loot. Thorbjorn returned to Orkney, where Earl Rognvald made up the difference by giving Thorbjorn money to cover the lost portion that Svein had claimed. Thorbjorn retaliated by declaring himself divorced from Svein's sister Ingigerd, and he sent her over to Svein in Caithness. Svein took this as a great insult. Earl Rognvald would later find himself leading a force against Svein Asleifsson, as Svein was raiding in the earl's land in Caithness. They were brought to terms by the intervention of King David I of Scotland, but it was obvious that Svein was becoming impossible to control.

In the spring of 1148 Earl Rognvald was invited to Norway by the sons of his friend King Harald Gilli, who now ruled the land between them. Rognvald made ready and sailed east to Bergen, accompanied by Earl Harald Maddadsson, who was then 14 years old. During their stay Eindridi the Younger returned home from Constantinople (Istanbul) with tales of the Holy Land. Earl Rognvald spent much time talking to Eindridi, who urged the earl to lead a pilgrimage to the Holy Land. This journey, Eindridi said, would bring him much honour and renown. A leading chieftain called Erling spoke in favour of the pilgrimage, and it was agreed that he would lead it with Rognvald and that Eindridi would be their guide. They would leave in two winters' time, and it was ordered that no one should have a ship of more than thirty benches for rowers except the earl, and that no ship but the earl's was to be ornamented. This was to prevent any jealousy arising between the men. Rognvald returned home and announced his plans of a pilgrimage to the Holy Land. Bishop William was to be the interpreter on the voyage, as he was a well educated man and spoke foreign languages.

In the spring of 1150 Rognvald entrusted the earldom to the teenage Earl Harald, and sailed east to Norway where Jon Limp-leg, his brother-in-law, had supervised the building of a ship of thirty five benches. The *Orkneyinga Saga* describes it as:

> ...a fine piece of workmanship, ornamented all over, and the figure-head and poop and weather-cocks inlaid with gold, and the rest of the ship carved from stem to stern.

Eindridi the Younger arrived, but he delayed their departure because the ship that he was having built wasn't ready. Eventually they set sail without him, the smaller ships remaining behind the earl's ship as a mark of respect. Suddenly, two large ships were seen heading towards them:

> One of the ships–a dragon ship–was richly ornamented. Both prow and poop were thickly inlaid with gold. The bows were painted, and it was painted all over from the gunwale to waterline wherever it seemed to look well.

The ship belonged to Eindridi. He had paid no heed to the earl's order regarding both size and ornamentation of the ships. They sailed on to Orkney, but Eindridi never arrived. News reached Earl Rognvald that Eindridi was in Shetland, and that his fine new ship had been wrecked there. Eindridi ordered another ship to be built, and it was decided to spend the winter in Orkney. During the winter there were many fights between the Norwegians and Orcadians *'over business and women'*.

In the summer of 1151 Earl Rognvald left Orkney at the head of fifteen ships. They sailed south past the east coast of Scotland and England, then to France. *Heimskringla* says that they sailed west, past the Hebrides and so on to Valland (France). Here they called in at Narbonne, where they heard that the earl who ruled there had died, leaving his estate to his only daughter, the young and beautiful Ermingard. Her advisers suggested that she invite Earl Rognvald and his leading men to a feast. Rognvald was captivated by her beauty, and she waited on him with golden cups filled with wine. He composed poems in honour of her beauty, and spent much of his time in her company. The townspeople were keen that they should marry, but Rognvald said that he had to continue with his pilgrimage, but he would call again on his way back.

They then sailed to Galicia in Spain, arriving there just before Yule. The local people were reluctant to trade with them, as they were short of food due to the oppression of a band of robbers who lived in a nearby castle. These robbers were led by a foreigner called Godfrey, a cunning and greedy man who was well educated and spoke many languages. The people of Galicia offered to trade with the earl and his men if they would attack the castle and kill their oppressors. This was agreed, and a market was set up. Earl Rognvald asked Erling Crick-neck how they should capture the castle. Erling said that he thought that the mortar in the walls of the castle looked weak, and that if they were to build a fire against the walls, then the mortar would crumble. They gathered wood to pile around the walls, but Bishop William prevented them from carrying out the attack until after Yule.

One night Godfrey had himself lowered over the castle wall on a rope. He was dressed in rags, and went around the earl's camp like a beggar. He saw that there were two factions led by Earl Rognvald and Eindridi the Younger. He saw how greedy and proud Eindridi was, and he managed to talk with him in secret. He said that he represented the chief in the castle, and offered him money if he would let the chief escape from the attack. After Yule the wood was placed along the castle walls and lit. The fire cracked the walls of the castle, leaving large breaches in them. Eindridi and his men were guarding the north side of the castle, which was obscured by smoke as the wind was blowing from the south. When Earl Rognvald's men entered the castle they killed many of the robbers, but gave peace to those who surrendered. There was no sign of the chief, and very little treasure was found. The suspicion fell on Eindridi, who had let Godfrey escape under the cover of the smoke into the nearby woods.

They continued their journey down the coast of Spain. Although it was supposed to be a pilgrimage, one could be forgiven for thinking that it was an old fashioned Viking raid. The *Orkneyinga Saga* says:

> They harried far and wide round the coast of heathen Spain, and got much booty there.

The ships were hit by strong winds, but they survived the storm. They then headed through the Straits of Gibraltar where Eindridi and his followers broke away from the earl's fleet and sailed to France with six ships. Earl Rognvald and his men saw this as being a confession of his guilt in letting Godfrey escape. The earl's ships carried on sailing along the coast of North Africa before being becalmed and engulfed by fog. One day the fog lifted and they saw two small islands rising from the sea in the distance. After a meal they noticed that one of the islands had disappeared. Earl Rognvald thought it likely that these were not islands at all, but huge merchant ships called dromonds. One must have caught a breeze, while the other was still becalmed. They had a meeting and decided to attack the ship. Erling Crick-neck suggested that they bring their ships close into the side of the dromond, as it was so large that the upper part of the hull would overhang them so that their missiles would fall into the sea beyond the earl's ships. They rowed to attack the ship, but the people on board showed no sign of fear and hung fine cloth and other goods over the side of the ship to taunt them.

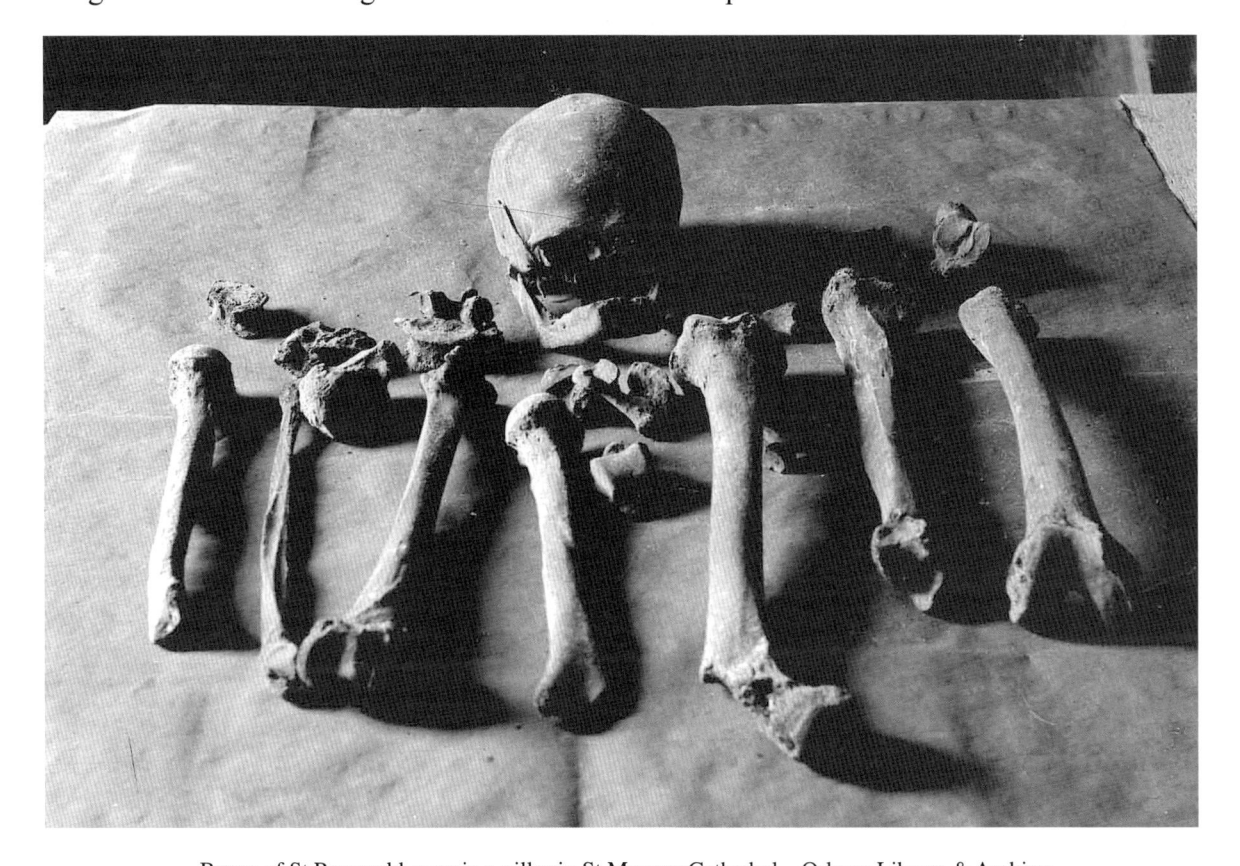

Bones of St Rognvald, now in a pillar in St Magnus Cathedral – Orkney Library & Archive

The ship was so high that the earl's men couldn't reach the upper deck with their weapons, but Rognvald took out his axe and began to cut his way through the side of the great ship. All the other men followed his example and began hacking into the hull with their axes, while Bishop William and the others lay off and fired arrows at the men on her deck as a distraction. When they had made holes large enough to climb through, Rognvald's men entered the ship and fought a hard battle with the dromond's crew. Erling received a wound on the neck that healed badly, which was the reason that he was known afterwards as Crick-neck. All of the men on the dromond were killed, except for one man who was taller and more handsome than the rest. Rognvald guessed that he must be a chief, and he ordered his men to press against him with their shields. He was surrounded and taken as a prisoner to the bishop's ship. He remained silent, but became agitated when the earl's men set fire to the dromond after they had looted it. As it blazed fiercely it seemed to them that a stream of gold or silver flowed from it. They realised then that they had not searched it well enough, and that a great deal of precious metal must have melted in the intense heat.

The earl sailed to a seaside market town in Serkland (the Viking name for Africa) and made a seven-day truce with the inhabitants so that they could trade with them. They tried to sell their captive, but nobody would buy him so Earl Rognvald gave him his freedom. The tall man left, but returned the following morning with a band of men and told Rognvald that he was a prince in Serkland, but he would spare their lives as they had treated him well. He said that they had indeed lost a great treasure of gold and silver when they burnt the dromond, and that he would be glad when they left as he never wanted to see them again.

The isle of Copinsay, Orkney from the sea – Drew Kennedy

They then sailed to Crete before they got a favourable wind that took them to the Holy Land. They stayed at Acre, where some of the men died of disease. Earl Rognvald visited all of the holy places and swam across the River Jordan with Sigmund Fish-hook, Svein Asleifsson's step-son. They both tied knots in some brushwood that grew there, and made verses shaming the people who had stayed at home by their firesides. This same incident is attributed to King Sigurd the Crusader when he made a pilgrimage to the Holy Land. *Heimskringla* tells how King Sigurd began to argue with his brother, King Eystein, while they were drinking. It was a custom to match man against man during drinking bouts, and King Eystein started to taunt his brother by boasting of his greatness. King Sigurd first listed the mighty deeds that he had done on his way to the Holy Land before issuing this challenge:

> Afterwards I travelled to our Lord's grave, and did not see thee there. On this voyage I came as far as the Jordan, where our Lord was baptised, and swam across the river; there I did not see thee either. On the other side of the river are some willow bushes. I tied a few of them into a knot and vowed that thou shouldst untie it. It is still waiting for thee down there and thou art called upon to fulfil this vow of mine.

It is interesting to note that the custom of twisting knots in brushwood to spite opponents is of Irish origin. It has been suggested that Earl Rognvald twisted the knots in imitation of King Sigurd, but Professor Bo Almqvist thinks that it is just as likely that Snorri Sturluson used this passage from the *Orkneyinga Saga* when he wrote *Heimskringla*. It is possible that a custom from the Celtic world could have reached Scandinavia via the Orkney earldom.[16]

Earl Rognvald and his men sailed to Constantinople in the autumn of 1152, where they were warmly welcomed by Emperor Manuel. They spent the winter there in great honour. Eindridi the Younger was also there with his men, but he had little good to say about the earl behind his back. The following spring they sailed to Bulgaria, then on to Puglia in Italy where they left their ships, taking horses instead and riding to Rome. They then set out northwards through Europe to Denmark before returning to Norway in the summer of 1153. Earl Rognvald won great fame because of this pilgrimage.

Erling Crick-neck and Eindridi the Younger would clash some ten years later during a period of civil war. Erling had become a powerful earl in Norway, marrying King Sigurd the Crusader's daughter Christina. Their son, Magnus, would later rule Norway before being defeated by King Sverri. Erling defeated an army led by an earl called Sigurd, killing both the earl and capturing Eindridi, who he put to death.

---

[16] Almqvist, Bo, *Viking Ale: Studies on Folklore Contacts between Northern and Western Worlds.* Boethius Press, Wales, 1991. p 22–23.

HOARDS

Vikings gathered riches, especially silver and gold, and sometimes they buried it. There have been more than thirty finds of Viking silver or gold in Scotland over the last four hundred years[1]. These treasures may have been hidden for safety, perhaps because there was some particular danger or perhaps because the owner was going away and wanted to be sure it would still be there when he came back. Some hoards might have been meant to stay in the ground. In *Ynglinga Saga*, Odin said that everyone coming into Valhalla should 'enjoy the use of what he himself had buried in the earth'. However, the saga was written in Iceland in the thirteenth century and it may not represent the beliefs held by Vikings in Orkney some two or three hundred years earlier.

There have been six finds of Viking silver and gold in Orkney. Each find is different, and some may not have been proper hoards at all. Two gold arm-rings said to have been found in the Broch of Burgar in Evie in 1840 may have been grave-goods with a skeleton, and the four gold rings found in Stenness in 1879 are small enough to have simply been lost by their original owner, rather than buried as a hoard.[2] Nothing is known of the nine silver arm-rings that were found "in a hillock near the Ring of Brodgar" sometime before 1700 and are now lost.[3]

A man digging peats near Caldale in about 1774 found a hoard of 300 coins and other silver, buried in two cow's horns. Some of the silver has been lost over the years but the coins that now remain are all from the reign of King Cnut of England, minted mostly in York, London, Lincoln or Stamford between about 1031 and 1035.[4] It seems possible that such a large unmixed group of coins was gathered together soon after the coins were minted, and it is tempting to link the hoard to Earl Thorfinn the Mighty, for it was about these years that he had the whole of Orkney under his control and was raiding down the coasts of Britain, presumably bringing back treasure. However, it is not known who gathered the Caldale hoard, or who buried it, or when, or why. It need not have anything to do with the few events and people that are recorded in the saga.

Vikings used silver as money, but they used it by weight rather than as coins. An arm-ring or a brooch fragment or a handful of Anglo-Saxon pennies would all be worth the same, if they weighed the same. Silver could be broken up, melted down and made into other objects without losing its value as "money". It is thought that some of the silver arm-rings from the hoards may have been "ring-money", perhaps given by the earls to their followers.

Burray Hoard – National Museums of Scotland

Stenness Hoard – National Museums of Scotland

The hoard found in the peat-moss in Burray in 1889 included 26 complete arm-rings and more than a hundred fragments, and a few coins. It is likely to have been buried sometime around the end of the tenth century or the beginning of the eleventh, perhaps in the latter days of the rule of Earl Sigurd the Stout. The hoard weighed almost two kilogrammes and was the second largest to have been found in Scotland, though it was less than a quarter of the size of the hoard from Skaill in Sandwick[5].

The Skaill hoard was found in March 1858. The first pieces were found near a rabbit-hole by a boy working the land. About a week later some neighbours went and found more. As much of the silver as possible was collected together by Orkney antiquarian George Petrie, who rewarded the finders and sent the hoard to Edinburgh. The find was declared Treasure Trove, and placed in the National Museum of Antiquities.

The hoard had coins, including one from Baghdad, along with pieces of hacksilver, armrings, beautiful twisted neck-rings and magnificent massive penannular brooches of a type most commonly found in the Viking areas around the Irish Sea. Four of these brooches share so many similarities that it seems most likely that many of them were made in the same workshop, possibly even all by one person[6]. Chemical analysis of the silver shows that they all have very similar compositions.[7]

The Skaill hoard as it is now weighs more than eight kilogrammes. It is the largest hoard known from Scotland. It is likely to have belonged to a very wealthy family, and was probably buried in the second quarter of the tenth century, around the time of Earl Thorfinn Skullsplitter.

Anne Brundle

[1] For details of all the Scottish hoards see Graham-Campbell, 1995.

[2] The arm-rings from Evie were said to be 'in the possession of the Earl of Zetland' in the middle nineteenth century, but are now lost (Graham-Campbell 1995, 103). The rings from Stenness are in the National Museum in Edinburgh (Graham-Campbell 1995, 130).

[3] Wallace 1700, *An Account of the Islands of Orkney* London

[4] Metcalf 1995, 24

[5] Graham-Campbell 1995, 131-141

[6] Graham-Campbell 1995, 35

[7] Wilthew 1995, 65

Caldale Hoard – National Museums of Scotland

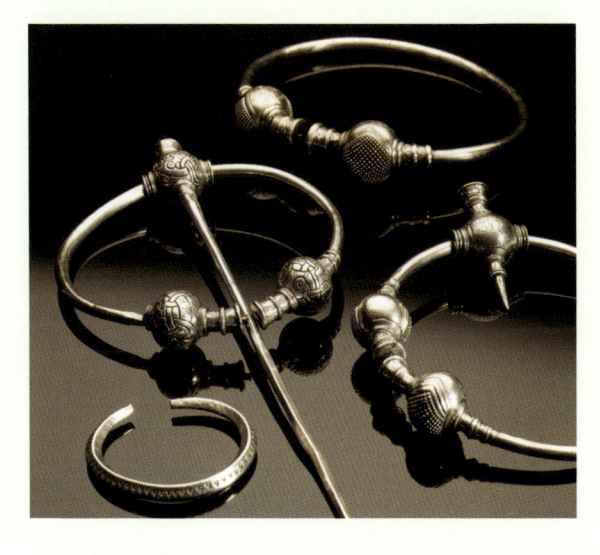

Skaill Hoard – National Museums of Scotland

The famous sea stack, The Old Man of Hoy, which would still have been attached to the mainland of Hoy at the time the Sagas were written – Raymond Parks

THE WAR OF THE THREE EARLS

The events in this chapter take place during the period 1151–1158. Erlend Haraldsson had a stronger claim to the earldom of Orkney than either Earl Rognvald Kali or Earl Harald Maddadsson, because his father had been earl. He joined forces with Svein Asleifsson and displaced Earl Harald from his position as joint earl. A series of allegiances was formed and broken as the three earls fought for control of the earldom of Orkney. Shortly after order is restored to the islands, Earl Rognvald was murdered by a former friend. Once more we see how lawless a society Orkney had become, when oaths and blood ties meant very little.

This period of civil war in Orkney is told in the *Orkneyinga Saga*. Erlend Haraldsson was the son of Earl Harald Smooth-tongue, the earl who had died when he put on the poisoned shirt. Of all the descendants of Earl Hakon Paulsson who thought they had a claim to the earldom of Orkney, Erlend had the strongest case. When he heard that Earl Rognvald had left Orkney on his voyage to the Holy Land he decided to act. He gained half of Caithness from the Scottish king, which his father had held before his death, then he made a claim for half of Orkney. His chief adviser was his foster-father, a man called Anakol. Earl Harald Maddadsson refused to share the earldom, but they called a truce for one year while Erlend sailed east to request his share of Orkney from King Eystein Haraldsson.

The excavation of the leet, at the Norse Mill, Bu, Orphir – Orkney Library & Archive

Things had not been going well for the young Earl Harald Maddadson. His father had died, and his mother Margaret had come to live with him in Orkney. Margaret was the daughter of Earl Hakon Paulsson. She was a very good-looking woman, and would cause trouble for Harald later. King Eystein had led a great force of eighty ships to raid Scotland during the summer of 1151. He heard that Earl Harald Maddadsson was in Thurso, so he took three cutters and caught the earl unawares. The king made Earl Harald swear loyalty to him, surrender his share of the Orkney earldom and ransom himself for three gold marks. In the autumn of the same year Harald's mother became pregnant to Gunni Olafsson, a brother of Svein Asleifsson. Harald had Gunni declared an outlaw, which led to a feud between him and Svein. This led to Svein forming an alliance with Erlend Haraldsson, despite the fact that Svein had burnt to death Erlend's grandmother Frakok.

On reaching Norway King Eystein granted Erlend the half of Orkney that belonged to Earl Harald Maddadsson. On Erlend's return to Orkney in September 1152 Svein Asleifsson advised that they take a force against Earl Harald before he heard of the king's decision from others. They sailed to Cairston near Stromness, where Earl Harald was on board his ship. On seeing the warships approach Harald and his men went ashore and ran into a castle that was there. One of Harald's men, Arni Hrafnsson, was so frightened that he ran all the way to Kirkwall with his shield slung over his back. He only realised that he was still wearing it when he became stuck in one of the cathedral's doors. A fierce battle raged until night with many wounded on both sides. The following morning the farmers went between the two sides and made peace. Earl Harald Maddadsson surrendered his half of Orkney and swore oaths never

Graemsay, with Stromness beyond – Keith Allardyce

to claim them again. He left Orkney with a few men and went to live in Scotland. The farmers swore oaths of loyalty to Earl Erlend, but upheld the right of Earl Rognvald to claim his half share of the islands should he return. They also swore that they would fight against Rognvald if he were to try to claim more than his half share.

Earl Harald returned to Orkney with four boats and twenty men in January 1153. The ships lay off Graemsay before landing at Hamnavoe (present day Stromness). Harald and his men headed towards Firth, where Erlend was staying, but a snow storm forced them to shelter for a night in the Neolithic tomb of Maeshowe (called Orkahaugr in the saga). Two of Harald's men went mad as a result of the night they spent in the tomb, which slowed them down. Earl Harald attacked the house where Earl Erlend had been staying, but Erlend had gone on board his ship for the night. Harald's men killed two of Erlend's followers and captured four others, including Arnfinn, the brother of Anakol, Erlend's foster-father. Earl Harald sent messengers demanding the ship that he had lost off Cairston in return for Arnfinn. Anakol led a raid against Earl Harald in Caithness and captured one of Harald's men, whom he successfully traded in return for his brother and the other captives.

In the spring of 1153 Earl Harald led a force to Shetland, as his mother had run off with a man called Erlend the Younger. Erlend the Younger had asked Earl Harald for his mother's hand in marriage, but he had been refused. They were now barricaded inside the Iron Age broch of Mousa, which was too well defended for Harald to capture. Men went between the two sides until Harald agreed to accept Erlend the Younger's proposal of help in return for marriage to his mother. This was not the only time that the Iron Age broch of Mousa was used as a sanctuary by lovers. In *Egil's Saga* (set in the ninth century) there is the story of a young man from Norway called Bjorn Brynjolfsson who carries off the beautiful Thora of the Embroidered Hand against the will of both of their fathers. They sail to Shetland where they marry and spend the winter in the broch tower of Mousa. King Harald Fair-hair issued orders to Earl Sigurd the Powerful, the first earl of Orkney, that Bjorn should be killed if he was caught, and this message was sent to the Hebrides and as far as Dublin. Bjorn and Thora sailed to Iceland instead, where they settled.

Earl Harald Maddadsson was in Norway when Earl Rognvald returned from the Holy Land. He heard how things stood in Orkney, and he wasted no time in returning to the islands. Men went between Earl Rognvald and Earl Erlend and brought about a peace meeting in Kirkwall where they agreed to share the islands and to defend them against Earl Harald. Earl Erlend and Svein Asleifsson sailed to Shetland to intercept all ships going to or coming from Norway, while Earl Rognvald sailed to Caithness because he thought it likely that Earl Harald would try to contact his relations there. Earl Harald sailed east from Norway with seven ships in the summer of 1154, but three were driven off course towards Shetland where they were captured. The remaining four ships arrived in Orkney where Earl Harald heard of the agreement between Earl Rognvald and Earl Erlend. He decided to seek out Rognvald in Caithness and try to strike a deal with him. Rognvald was attending his daughter Ingirid's marriage to Erik Stay-brails when he heard of Harald's arrival, and he set off at the head of a large group of men. Erik was a kinsman of Harald's, and he and several other men persuaded Rognvald to join with him against Earl Erlend. The two earls met and agreed to form an alliance against Erlend.

Earl Rognvald and Earl Harald sailed to Orkney where Earl Erlend and Svein Asleifsson were in South Ronaldsay. Svein's spies saw that the two earls were now in partnership and reported back to him. He said that they couldn't fight both earls, so they sailed to Caithness and raided there. That winter Svein and Erlend returned to Orkney and found out that Rognvald and Harald were at Scapa with fourteen ships. Earl Rognvald had set off for his hall in Orphir, but was forced to shelter from a heavy sleet shower at the farm of Knarston. Svein and Earl Erlend attacked the ships so suddenly that many of Earl Harald's men were killed and Harald himself was forced to leap over the side of his ship to escape. Svein learnt that Earl Rognvald was at Knarston and set off for the farm with a band of warriors. They were met at the door of the farm by Botolf Bungle, the Icelandic skald who lived there. They asked if Earl Rognvald was there, but Botolf answered in verse that Rognvald and his men had gone shooting wild fowl in the hills. When Svein had left, Botolf went to wake Rognvald who was asleep inside. Earl Rognvald headed for his hall in Orphir where he found Earl Harald in hiding. They both made good their escape by sailing to Caithness in small boats.

Just before Yule, Svein Asleifsson went to settle a dispute between a kinswoman and her neighbour in Sandwick. Earl Erlend had gone to Damsay where he sat drinking in the hall that was there. When Svein heard this he sent a message to Erlend advising him to spend his nights aboard his ships, as he suspected an attack from the two earls. Erlend's men were dismissive of Svein's words and continued to drink in the hall, but the earl and some of his men went aboard ship for the night. That very night, 21st December 1154, Earl Rognvald and Earl Harald made a surprise attack on Earl Erlend's ship. One of his men tried to wake Erlend, but he was so drunk that he couldn't be roused. The man picked him up in his arms and jumped over the side of the ship and landed in a small boat that was there. There was confusion among Erlend's men, and they surrendered to Rognvald and Harald. A search was made for Erlend's body, which wasn't found until 23rd December when a spear shaft was seen sticking out of a heap of seaweed. They found that the spear had been driven through Earl Erlend's body. His men were given peace, and Erlend's body was carried to St Magnus Cathedral in Kirkwall where he was buried in one of the walls. His grave can be seen to the east of the south transept.

Earl Rognvald sent a message to Svein Asleifsson that he wanted to spend Yule with him, and that he wanted his friendship. Svein and Rognvald spent Yule together on good terms, but Rognvald still had to bring about a settlement between Svein and Harald. It was agreed that Svein was to pay a gold mark each to Rognvald and Harald and surrender half of his land and his good longship. Rognvald refused to accept Svein's payment to him, but Harald treated him and his estate badly. It ended with Svein attacking Harald's men at his home in Gairsay and then fleeing from Harald's ships. Svein hid his ship from Harald in a sea cave as he was escaping to Sanday. The saga says that this was on *Hellis eyjar* (Hellis Isle), possibly Muckle Green Holm, which has two large sea caves on its eastern side. Earl Rognvald again intervened and brought peace between Svein and Harald, but it was an uneasy truce.

On 27th May 1155, Earl Rognvald held peace talks between Svein and Harald, and they came to terms. The great sail of the longship that Svein had paid as compensation had been stored in St Magnus Cathedral, and he frowned as he saw it being carried out. Earl Harald invited Svein to come and talk to him, which he did, despite Rognvald's warning of possible danger. Harald gave Svein the longship and returned his lands to him, as well as other goods confiscated by the earl's men. Svein and Harald were at peace after that, and Svein spent a lot of his time with Earl Rognvald.

Later that winter, a dispute arose between the followers of Earl Rognvald and Thorbjorn Clerk, Earl Harald's foster-father and chief counsellor. Despite both the earls' efforts, Thorbjorn continued the feud and killed one of Rognvald's men. Earl Rognvald had Thorbjorn declared an outlaw and banished from his lands. Thorbjorn went to the court of King Malcolm IV of Scotland, but sometimes he stayed with friends in Caithness. There was no love lost between him and Earl Rognvald.

The earls used to go deer hunting in Caithness during the summer. In August 1158 they heard news that Thorbjorn Clerk had gathered a group of men and intended to attack Earl Rognvald. The earls raised a gathering of one hundred men, twenty mounted and eighty on foot. They arrived at the farm of Hallvard Dufasson at Forsie in Calder Dale. Earl Rognvald rode at the head of his men. Hallvard was building a stack; one translation says it was corn, a second oats, and a third hay.[17] When Hallvard saw Earl Rognvald, he shouted to him by name, and asked him for news. This alerted Thorbjorn Clerk and his men who were sitting inside drinking, and they armed themselves ready for an attack. They pulled down stones that filled a concealed

The Crossing, St Magnus Cathedral, Kirkwall – Raymond Parks

[17] (1) Hjaltalin, Jon A. and Goudie, Gilbert. 1873. (2) Taylor, Alexander Burt. 1938. (3) Pálsson, Hermann and Edwards, Paul. 1978.

doorway and took up position by a wall next to a narrow lane that led up to the house. As Earl Rognvald rode up the lane Thorbjorn struck at him with his sword, but the blow was blocked by a young man called Asolf who lost a hand as a result. The sword wounded Rognvald on the chin and caused him to fall from his horse. His foot became stuck in the stirrup, and a man called Stephen thrust a spear at him. Thorbjorn again struck him with his sword, but received a serious wound as a spear was thrust upwards through his thigh and into his belly. Thorbjorn was able to escape with his men, heading up higher to where there was marshy ground.

When Earl Harald came on the scene he was urged to go after Thorbjorn Clerk, but he tried to stall for time, saying that he would wait to see what Earl Rognvald advised. Harald was not keen to see his foster-father killed. As Earl Rognvald lay dying, his men set off in pursuit of Thorbjorn, who had by this time crossed the marsh with around fifty men. The earl's men were on the other side of the marsh, and they threw spears at Thorbjorn and his followers. Thorbjorn ordered that no spears should be thrown back, and when things had calmed down he asked Earl Harald for peace. He said that he had done much in his honour and that the killing of Earl Rognvald would only increase his power, as Rognvald had treated him no better than a page-boy. Earl Harald was starting to be swayed by Thorbjorn's speech, until Magnus Havardsson spoke out against him. He was the highest ranking man among Earl Rognvald's party, and he gave Earl Harald a stark warning. He said that if Harald gave Thorbjorn peace then people would think that he too was implicated in the murder. Thorbjorn had already as good as said that he had done the killing in order to increase Harald's power and fame, and if the killing was unavenged then it would seem as if Harald was part of the plot.

Earl Erlend's burial place, St Magnus Cathedral – Orkney Library & Archive

When Harald saw what people were thinking he leapt across the marsh in full armour, a distance of nine ells (thirteen and a half feet). His men followed, but none of them cleared the marsh in one leap. Thorbjorn's followers fled, but he tried one last time to get peace from Earl Harald. Thorbjorn went to Earl Harald and got down on his knees and pleaded for his life. Harald told him to run away, as he wouldn't fight against his own men in order to defend him. Thorbjorn and eight of his men sought safety in a small house, but it was set alight and as it collapsed they were forced to run outside where they were all killed. When Thorbjorn's body was examined they found that his intestines had slipped out through the spear wound that he had received when he attacked Rognvald.

Earl Rognvald died on 20th August 1158. His body was taken back to Orkney and a tomb was made for him in St Magnus Cathedral. Miracles were attributed to him, and he was made a saint in 1192.

ORPHIR

The Bu at Orphir has been the scene for several exciting episodes in the *Orkneyinga Saga*. These include the poisoned shirt incident whereby Earl Harald Smoothtongue put on a poisoned shirt intended for his half brother and the "two Sveins" episode where Svein Asleifsson killed Svein Breistrope after a drunken dispute; it was also a place of refuge for Earl Rognvald and Earl Harald Maddadsson when they were attacked by Earl Erlend and Svein Asleifsson.

Bu is the name given to several farms in Orkney - all of high status and most of them part of the Earldom estate. This Bu was a home farm for the Earl, at which they often spent Yule. Here, at Bu, Orphir, the archaeological site itself is now mostly invisible, and preserved beneath fields, car park and farm buildings, but it is known to cover an extensive area. The most prominent feature here is the ruins of the round church dedicated to St Nicholas. It was thought to have been built by Earl Hakon Paulsson (killer of St Magnus) following his repentant return from his pilgrimage to the Holy Land and Rome. It is thought possible that the design of this church was inspired by the Holy Sepulchre in Jerusalem. A rune stone found in the church praises it, translated by expert runologist Michael Barnes as saying "no church is as pleasing to God as [this]". In 1757 most of the church was demolished.

A magnate farm would have consisted of many different elements; here, the remains of the leet and pit for a horizontal water mill have been

The Round Church dedicated to St Nicholas, Bu, Orphir – Raymond Parks

found. The wheel which drives the grinding stones is turned horizontally, powered by a stream passing over its paddles. Often, more than one mill will be found on a single stream. In other places at the Earl's Bu, masses of burnt stone have been found. These stones are the refuse left by a method of heating water by roasting stones in a fire and then dropping them into tanks of water. At the Brough of Birsay, the material was associated with a room in the Norse settlement, and interpreted as a bath house or sauna.

Various excavations over the years have identified many remains of the era, but a very extensive excavation would need to be done before it would be possible to be sure which hall had been found. The drinking hall of the Earl would have been near the church, but it is not known exactly where this lies. The Earl's hall would have been a large establishment, which he would have required for entertaining his large retinue and his important guests, together with their followers. The hall is described in the *Orkneyinga Saga*:

The Click Mill, Dounby – Raymond Parks

There was a great drinking-hall at Orphir, with a door in the south wall near the eastern gable, and in front of the hall, just a few paces down from it, stood a fine church. On the left as you came into the hall was a large stone slab, with a lot of big ale vats behind it, and opposite the door was the living room.

The stone slab would probably have been set on edge, and, with the barrels, it provided the notorious Svein Asleifsson with his cover for jumping out and killing Svein Breistrope with an axe.

Julie Gibson

The Bu, Orphir – Raymond Parks

Views of modern Stromness – Raymond Parks

THE DEATH OF SVEIN ASLEIFSSON

The events in this chapter take place during the period 1158–c1171. Svein Asleifsson continued to dominate Orkney as a mighty chieftain, who rivalled the earl in wealth and power. He died a true Viking's death, sword in hand and defiant to the end. With his passing Orkney finally shook off the old ways of the Viking age, which had actually ended a century before.

What we know of Svein Asleifsson comes from the *Orkneyinga Saga*. Svein Asleifsson enjoyed great fame and power and even fostered Earl Harald Maddadsson's son Hakon. Svein lived in his great hall in Gairsay where he kept eighty warriors at his own expense, as well as servants and his own family. His hall was the largest in Orkney, bigger even than the earl's. The present day house on Gairsay, dating from the seventeenth century, is called Langskaill (meaning the long hall) and is thought to be on the site of Svein's great drinking hall. Although what we call the Viking era had passed, Svein still maintained that way of life. In the spring he would sow his crops, and then set out with several ships to raid in the Hebrides and Ireland. This he called his 'spring Viking-cruise'. He returned to Gairsay to harvest his crop, and then he set out on his 'autumn Viking-cruise' before winter.

Around the year 1171 Svein had a highly successful spring viking-cruise, raiding in the Hebrides, the Isle of Man and Ireland. He captured two English ships which yielded a large

Gairsay – Jim Scott

quantity of broad-cloth. The merchants were left with only the clothes that they stood up in, while Svein sailed away with their ships and goods. When they returned to Orkney, Svein had the broad-cloth sewn onto the sails of the ships so that they made a great show as they sailed home to Gairsay. Svein unloaded the plunder from his ships, which included wine and English mead. He invited Earl Harald to a feast and entertained him in great style. During the evening Harald asked Svein to give up raiding, as he was getting on in years and he was concerned that he would meet a violent death. Svein said that he was feeling his age, and that *'wet work and warring'* were taking their toll on him. He wanted to go on one last raid, to try to see if his autumn viking-cruise would be as successful as the spring one had been. Earl Harald replied:

> It is hard to tell, comrade, which will come first, death or lasting fame.

That autumn Svein Asleifsson set out with seven large ships and raided the Hebrides, but he got little in the way of plunder. He sailed as far as Dublin, where he took the inhabitants by surprise, entering the town with his men and ransacking the place. He took the leading members of the town as hostages and made the Dubliners swear oaths that they would surrender the town to him. He was to return the following morning to gather gold and to put his own men in charge of the town. That night the Dubliners dug pits inside the town gates and in other places where Svein and his men would walk, and then they covered them over with branches and straw. The following morning Svein and his men marched up to the town gates, but instead of receiving the surrender of the town they fell into the pits and were trapped. The Dubliners

Eynhallow – Orkney Museums and Heritage

attacked the helpless men, killing every last one of them. It was said that Svein Asleifsson was the last to die, shouting defiantly and brandishing his sword. The remaining men who stayed with the ships returned to Orkney with the news of Svein's death. His sons divided up his estate between them, and divided the long hall into separate homes for themselves.

HORSES

The Mainland of Orkney was called *Hrossey* by the saga-writers, meaning 'horse-island.' Horses feature strongly in the Icelandic sagas but are only mentioned incidentally in the *Orkneyinga Saga*. For example, in the twelfth century there is young Svein Asleifsson who escaped on horseback from Orphir across the hills after murdering Svein Breast-rope at Earl Paul's Christmas feast,[1] or Ragna from North Ronaldsay who wore a head-dress made from horse-hair when she went to ask a favour of Earl Rognvald Kali Kolsson.[2]

Horses were kept to be ridden, to carry goods and to pull loads. Viking-period horses were generally smaller than modern horses, more like large ponies, so it may actually be true that Hrolf the Ganger got his name because he was too big to ride a horse and had to walk everywhere.[3]

In pre-Christian times horse-meat could be eaten, but perhaps it seldom was because horse-bones have not commonly been found in household middens of any period. Artefacts made of horse bone are found in excavations of Viking period sites in Britain. Most of the artefacts are made of metapodials, the lower leg bones that might be left with the hide when an animal was skinned, so the raw material for these artefacts could have come from tanneries.[4]

Very few traces of horses have been found in excavations in Orkney. Archaeological excavations concentrate on buildings, or on the middens made of the waste created by the household and by the animals that were kept indoors during the winter. Horse carcasses are not likely to have been left in these places for if horses were slaughtered, whether because of old age or for their skins, the remains would probably not have been close to the house.

Horse harness is mostly made from perishable materials which do not survive, such as leather, held together by metal fastenings which are hard to identify on their own. One of the few pieces from Orkney is a snaffle bit that was found in excavations at Burnside in Birsay in the 1970s[5]. It has a mouthpiece made in two parts, and ring-shaped cheek-pieces. It is a very common type of bit and could date from almost any time in the last thousand years, but it is most likely to be Norse because it was found in a midden with other Norse period artefacts. A similar bit was found in a Viking grave at Reay in Caithness[6].

Horses are sometimes found buried with their owners in Viking graves. Pagan Vikings were buried with jewellery, weapons, household goods and other possessions appropriate to their social position or wealth, and sometimes these included animals. In 1788 the Reverend George Low noted bones of horses and dogs amongst the other grave goods found in Viking graves that had been uncovered by storms at Pierowall in Westray.[7] Excavation there in the next century discovered at least seventeen graves in the Links, almost all accompanied by grave-goods, and three of which contained horses. Two of the horses had been buried with their bits still between their teeth.[8]

Anne Brundle

A snaffle-bit from horse harness
– Orkney Museums and Heritage

[1] Taylor 1938, 244, ch 66

[2] Taylor 1938, 268, ch 81

[3] Hrolf the Ganger was the conqueror of Normandy and thus ancestor of the Kings of England. He was one of the brothers of Earl Torf-Einar. Taylor 1938, 138, ch 4

[4] Macgregor 1985, 31

[5] Morris, C D 1996, 61

[6] Greig 1940, Fig 5, 21

[7] Graham-Campbell and Batey 1998, 129

[8] Graham-Campbell and Batey 1998, 133

Iceland horse in a wintry landscape in Iceland
– Àsborg Arnþossdóttir

Eight-legged Sleipnir, thought to be carrying a dead man
– detail from the Lärbro stone, Gotland

Bishop's Palace, Kirkwall – Raymond Parks

EARL HARALD MADDADSSON AND THE LOSS OF SHETLAND

The events in this chapter take place during the period 1158–1214. Earl Harald Maddadsson continued to rule as sole earl of Orkney, despite the challenge from Earl Rognvald's grandson, Harald the Younger, who had the backing of both the Norwegian and Scottish crowns. After defeating and killing Harald the Younger, Earl Harald Maddasson found himself having to submit to the demands of the Scottish king. He also lost control of Shetland when he backed an unsuccessful attempt to overthrow King Sverri of Norway. From this point onwards the earldom of Orkney was losing its position of influence and power in the Nordic world. It was a pale shadow of its former glory when Earl Thorfinn the Mighty ruled over a huge realm.

After the death of Earl Rognvald Kali, Earl Harald Maddadsson ruled all of Orkney by himself. The *Orkneyinga Saga* describes him as being *'...a great chief, the tallest and strongest of men, obstinate and hard-hearted.'* Earl Rognvald Kali had only one child, his daughter Ingirid who married Erik Stay-brails. They had three sons, Harald the Younger, Magnus Mangi and Rognvald. These three men went to Norway where King Magnus (the son of Erling Crick-neck who went on the pilgrimage with Earl Rognvald) gave Harald the Younger the title of earl of Orkney, and half of the islands. Harald the Younger then went to King William the

Interior of Eynhallow Church, Eynhallow – Pete Stokes

Lion of Scotland and was granted half of the earldom of Caithness, which his grandfather Earl Rognvald had previously ruled. This took place in the year 1198. Harald the Younger gathered together a force of men in Caithness, then sent a message to Earl Harald Maddadsson (now called 'Harald the Elder') asking him to share power. Earl Harald Maddadsson refused to divide his realm and sent the messengers away with insults. Earl Harald Maddadsson raised a great army and a fleet of ships to carry the men to Caithness. Harald the Younger sent his brother-in-law, Lifolf Bald-pate, over to Orkney to spy on Earl Harald Maddadsson. He saw a great fleet ready to sail off South Ronaldsay and hurried back to warn Harald the Younger. Soon Earl Harald Maddadsson's fleet was sighted heading for Caithness. Harald the Younger decided to stand and fight, although he was heavily outnumbered.

The two armies clashed in a bloody and hard fought battle. Harald the Younger's army fought valiantly, but being so outnumbered their leaders started to fall and eventually Harald the Younger was also killed. He fell by the side of some peat cuttings, and it was said that where his blood was spilt a great light shone at night. A church was later built on the site, and miracles were claimed to have occurred there. It was said that he should have been made a saint, and that his spirit wanted his remains to be taken over to Orkney to lie beside St Magnus and St Rognvald.

Earl Harald Maddadsson now claimed all of Caithness for himself. When King William the Lion of Scotland heard of the death of Harald the Younger, and that Earl Harald Maddadsson had claimed Caithness without asking him he grew angry and raised an army to avenge the insult. The king's force was drawn from Scotland, the Hebrides and Ireland. Earl Harald Maddadsson remained in Orkney while the king's army re-took Caithness. King William set

Exterior of Eynhallow Church, Eynhallow – Pete Stokes

three stewards over Caithness, but Harald sent an assassin who killed one of them. Around the year 1201 Earl Harald Maddadsson led a great force to Caithness to claim it back. His men surrounded a fortress that was at Scrabster, but Bishop Jon of Caithness tried to make peace between the two sides. Earl Harald listened to him for a while, then he ordered him to be seized and his tongue cut out and a knife driven into each eye. It was said that his sight and the power of speech was returned to him by the intervention of St Triduana (St Tredwell). Earl Harald then drove the stewards from the land and forced all the Caithness men to swear an oath of loyalty to him.

King William was furious, and he raised a huge army and marched north to attack Earl Harald. The army camped on the borders between Sutherland and Caithness and it was so huge that their tents filled an entire valley. Harald raised an army of 6000 men, but it was nowhere near large enough to take on the king's force. Messengers were sent to the king to ask for peace. The king was reluctant to give it, but he eventually agreed to a peace deal in return for a fourth of the income from Caithness. This demand was brought back to Harald, who agreed to the terms. He returned to Orkney, but he had managed to hold on to Caithness, albeit with a reduced income.

A few years earlier, in 1194, Earl Harald had lost Shetland to King Sverri of Norway. Not much is said about this in the *Orkneyinga Saga,* as the latter part of the saga was written around the time of Earl Harald's death and portrayed him in a favourable light. There is much more detail in *Sverri's Saga,* which was told from the other side's point of view. Sverri was born in Norway but raised in the Faeroes. He was training for the priesthood, but one night he had a dream that he had become a bird so huge that it covered all of Norway. His mother made a pilgrimage to Rome, where she confessed that the father of her son was King Sigurd of Norway, the son of King Harald Gilli. This information was brought to the Pope who ordered her to go back to the Faeroes and tell her son the truth about his parentage. She did so, and Sverri sailed to Norway with hopes of gaining the throne.

He soon discovered that the people of Norway preferred to have a descendant of King Sigurd the Crusader as their king rather than a descendant of King Harald Gilli. King Magnus, the son of Earl Erling Crick-neck, was now on the throne and proved to be a popular ruler. A band of desperate warriors adopted Sverri as their leader, and they spent several years travelling through Norway and fighting against King Magnus and his father, Earl Erling Crick-neck. Sverri's band of warriors had experienced severe hardship and had at one point resorted to wrapping birch bark around their legs to keep them warm, so people called them the 'birch-legs'. Earl Erling Crick-neck was killed in a battle at Nidaros (Trondheim) in 1179, and was buried there with honour. King Magnus was killed in battle against Sverri at Norafjord near Bergen in 1184. Magnus Mangi, Earl Rognvald Kali's grandson and brother of Harald the Younger, was also killed there with King Magnus. King Sverri was now the sole ruler of Norway.

Earl Harald Maddadsson's son-in-law, Olaf Earl's-kin, was involved in a plot to put a boy called Sigurd Kingsson on the throne of Norway. The boy was the son of the late King Magnus

Erlingsson and had been fostered by Olaf. Along with Olaf in this plot was Hallkel Jonsson, who was married to Ragnhild, King Magnus's sister. Olaf Earl's-kin managed to gain King Sverri's trust before carrying the boy off to Shetland. The following spring they sailed south to Orkney and stayed with Earl Harald Maddadsson. When the plot to put the boy on the Norwegian throne was revealed to the earl he supported it. *Sverri's Saga* is in no doubt about the earl's role in the rebellion:

> The Earl supported the boy's cause heartily and gave him a good long-ship, for King Magnus had been an excellent friend of Earl Harald. The Earl also gave leave to all who wished to join the expedition of Hallkel and Olaf and their companions.

In 1193 the expedition was ready to sail to Norway:

> A great multitude now gathered around him from the Orkneys and Shetland, and having procured ships, they started from the west in the summer.

They sailed to Tunsberg where they captured and killed King Sverri's nephew, Jon. They had Sigurd Kingsson proclaimed king before sailing to Oslo. This group was called the *Eyskeggs*, meaning the 'island beards,' but they called themselves the 'golden-legs,' as opposed to the more humble 'birch-legs' of King Sverri. They continued to gather men to their army so that King Sverri's men were in too weak a position to fight them. The *Eyskeggs* sailed to Bergen where they spent the winter.

In the spring of 1194 King Sverri sailed from Trondheim to Bergen. The *Eyskeggs* had gathered their ships together in Floruvoe ready to do battle. King Sverri had spied on their movements and knew that they were preparing to attack with the dawn. He rallied his men by saying that they would attack before light and so that they could recognise each other they would tie strips of linen to the prows of their ships. King Sverri had twenty ships, but they were rather small. The *Eyskeggs* had fourteen ships, mostly large vessels. Towards morning the *Eyskeggs* sailed out to look for Sverri's ships. When the two sides met they raised a war-cry and joined battle. The fighting was fierce, but the *Eyskeggs* had the advantage of higher ships. They attacked King Sverri's ship, killing the forecastle men and capturing the king's standard. King Sverri's men cut the ropes from the grappling-hooks and seemed to be about to flee. The *Eyskeggs* cut their ropes to pursue them, but the strong current broke up the formation of the ships so that they were scattered. King Sverri took advantage of this by attacking the larger ships with two or three smaller ones. Reinforcements came to King Sverri's aid, and the tide of the battle now turned against the *Eyskeggs* as ship after ship was cleared of men. Sigurd Kingsson leapt over the side of his ship, but was killed in the water. Olaf Earl's-kin also swam for the shore, but he was killed by King Sverri's followers as he waded out of the sea. Hallkel Jonsson died with most of his men fighting on board his ship.

King Sverri gave quarter to the *Eyskeggs* who remained alive, but most had been killed. He celebrated by having a mass sung, then he showed the bodies of Sigurd Kingsson and Olaf Earl's-kin as proof that they were dead. Sigurd Kingsson was buried in Maria Kirk, Bergen, while the *Eyskeggs* were buried in a mass grave. Olaf Earl's-kin's body was placed on top of his fallen warriors in the grave.

The following summer there was a great meeting of Bishops in Bergen. Among them was Bishop Bjarni from Orkney, the son of Kolbein Hruga (Kolbein Heap, a powerful chieftain who lived in Wyre and whose great size resulted in him becoming associated with the giant 'Cubbie Roo' of Orcadian folklore). Along with Bishop Bjarni were Earl Harald Maddadsson and the leading men from Orkney. It had become known to them that King Sverri intended to send an army west to punish the Orcadians for their treason. Bishop Bjarni thought it wise to use the meeting of bishops as an excuse for bringing Earl Harald and his men to see the king. A meeting was held between Earl Harald Maddadsson and King Sverri in the yard in front of Christ Kirk. The king was there with a large following, while the earl stood facing him with his own men. Earl Harald now had to speak to save his life and his earldom.

> There is now assembled here a large number of good men, and I may need in my speech much encouragement from the people. I am now an old man, as you can see from my beard. I have drawn near to the knees of many kings, sometimes with much affection, and often in difficult circumstances. Now there is a new difficulty on my hands, the anger of

Cubbie Roo's Castle, Wyre – Gunnie Moberg

my lord, King Sverri. Less blame is mine in this business than is imputed to me. I did not plan the rising of that band. It is true that I did not fight against it, for I could not be hostile to all the people in the land as long as I should be Earl over it. The men of Orkney do not always act as I wish; many leave the Orkneys to plunder in Ireland and Scotland, to pillage merchants, and all contrary to my wish. And yet people say that I am not slow to punish. But there is no need here to speak long, as the thing has been done; I commit all into God's hands and yours Sire.

Earl Harald Maddadsson then went before King Sverri and fell at his feet. The king made a speech saying how much destruction had been done in his land by the *Eyskeggs*, but that he was prepared to forgive the earl as he had come to him and submitted to his power. The punishment was to be that every estate owned by those who fought for the *Eyskeggs* was forfeited to the crown, unless the family paid a ransom to the king within three years. He also took Shetland into royal control, but left Earl Harald in charge of Orkney.

Earl Harald Maddadsson died in Orkney in 1206. He was succeeded by his sons John and David, with John ruling solely after David's death in 1214. Earl Harald Maddadsson had been earl of Orkney for twenty years with Earl Rognvald, and was sole ruler for another forty-eight years after Rognvald's death.

St Mary's Kirk, Wyre, which dates from the twelfth century – Raymond Lamb

A piece of chain mail found beneath the floor of St Mary's Kirk, Wyre – Orkney Library & Archive

The present day Bu, Wyre, which is thought to lie over the remains of Kolbein Hruga's hall – Orkney Library & Archive

WESTRAY

Westray is Viking territory, and Pierowall lies at its heart. It is described in the *Orkneyinga Saga* as a village or *thorp* named for its haven or harbour. Until sand blows infilled some of the bay in the last couple of hundred years, Pierowall was on a very narrow neck of land, which would have been suitable for portage to the North – when the winds were not suitable to sail around Westray, Viking boats could have been dragged a short way across land instead. Its geographical position as Orkney's first and last harbour on the Shetland sea route would have been significant. It seems that Pierowall was originally a Viking settlement, possibly a trading station, which grew into a village by the twelfth century.

Pierowall was in fact Earl Rognvald's first stop in Orkney. He arrived from Shetland with his war band, required allegiance, and attended Mass at the church in Pierowall. Standing outside, he made up a humorous verse about the unusual style of dress and hair sported by a large group of priests, and suggested that their appearance was a bit effeminate! The church mentioned in the Saga is surely Lady Kirk, which lies close to the shore at the head of the bay in the village. This church will have its roots solidly in the Norse period, although it was so altered in the seventeenth century that this is now difficult to discern. The clerics in question may have been from Papa Westray, one of two islands in the sagas named Papa for their priests, that lies just a short boat journey away across the harbour. Perhaps they came from a monastery at St Boniface, where a Norse hog-back tombstone (a house-shaped Christian grave-stone) can still be found at the beautifully restored medieval church.

The story of Pierowall goes back some hundreds of years before the time of the Sagas, however. Pierowall is the site of the largest pagan Viking cemetery yet to be discovered in the British Isles. Here in the dunes around the village (but no one is entirely sure exactly where) were the graves of many – at least twenty – pagan Vikings. Vikings were buried with the essential goods for their after-life, including knives, sickles, ornaments such as brooches and their weapons. A lurid report, written in Russia by an Arab trader who observed the funeral rituals of a Viking chieftain, describes, amongst other things, the way in which a slave-woman was killed to accompany her dead master into the after-life. Whilst there are other explanations for a single burial of several individuals, this evidence of

Cross Kirk – Vicky Szabo

Excavations at Quoygrew revealed a longhouse that was lived in and modified from the twelfth – sixteenth centuries – 59° North/Frank Bradford

Excavations at Tuquoy revealed a high status twelfth-century hall, probably the home of Thorkill Flayer – Raymond Lamb.

sacrifice makes possible the consideration that the two individuals (a child and a man) who accompanied the elderly Viking lady buried in Scar in Sanday may have been slaves sacrificed for the purpose. At Pierowall the detail of the graves is absent, because the nineteenth-century excavators were more interested in the grave-goods than anything else. They revealed burials, however, some reported to have been under cairns and others in cists (or stone boxes). There were graves of women as well as men. One grave included the Viking's horse. No doubt it was made ready for his use in the afterlife. Dogs were also sacrificed. The way the graves are spread out here and there across the land at the back of Pierowall is very reminiscent of other Viking trading settlements in Scandinavia. Raymond Lamb and others have suggested that Pierowall was a Viking trading emporium which was eventually superceded by Kirkwall.

Just outside Pierowall lies the Viking and Norse site of Quoygrew. Here, archaeologists have discovered that a single long-house started in the time of the Sagas grew, through room being added end on to room, over some 600 years. During the occupation of this site, the changes in lifestyle from the Pictish people, to the Vikings and the Christian Norse, through to the eventual Scottification of Orkney can all be read in the material excavated by James Barrett.

A high status farm and its associated chapel lay at the southern shore of Westray. These probably represent the farm of the unpopular Saga figure, Thorkell Flettir. In Orkney the sea is rising slowly in comparison with the land. This results in a lot of damage to hundreds of archaeological sites. Lack of government funding means that most suffer depredation without any form of detailed record being made. Luckily, this has not been entirely the case here, and some limited excavation has been undertaken. A massive stone structure was discovered and some of it excavated, probably a hall, and of the right date to belong to Thorkell or his son Haflidi. Along the cliff edge many more structures and middens (rubbish heaps) can be seen, extending for some 50m. Standing on the beach it is possible to understand how big this settlement was. The nearby church, Cross Kirk, would have dated to the time of the Sagas. It is now a roofless but charming ruin. In Thorkell's day it would probably have been lime-plastered, and bright wall-paintings would probably have enlivened the interior. Luckily the chapel is safe from the sea, and beautifully kept in State care, at least for the foreseeable future.

Julie Gibson

Detail of 'Gaia' in Kirkwall Harbour – Drew Kennedy

KING HAKON HAKONSSON, THE LAST OF THE GREAT SEA-KINGS

The events in this chapter take place during the period 1202–1266. King Hakon the Old was the last of the Norwegian sea-kings. He increased his power by annexing Iceland and Greenland, but his final struggle against the Scottish king ended in failure and saw the beginning of the end of Norwegian rule over the Scottish islands. Orkney was moving closer to Scotland, especially after the death of Earl John Haraldsson and his heirs, when the earldom of Orkney passed to a Scottish family.

The story of King Hakon Hakonsson is told in *Hakon's Saga*. King Sverri died on 9th March 1202 and was succeeded by his son, King Hakon. King Hakon's rule was short, because he died on New Year's Day 1203. King Hakon had no legitimate heirs, but he did have an illegitimate son who was born a few months after the king died and was named Hakon Hakonsson after his late father. This Hakon would later be adopted as king by the 'birch-legs', the warriors who were still loyal to the young Hakon's late grandfather, King Sverri. Hakon Hakonsson shared power with Earl Skuli, and later cemented the alliance by marrying Skuli's daughter. His history, *Hakonarsaga* (Hakon's Saga), was written by Sturla Thordarsson, the nephew of the great saga writer Snorri Sturluson. Ironically, Sturla had been summoned to Norway to face King Hakon's wrath after speaking against him becoming the sovereign ruler of Iceland. He won the affection of King Hakon's son, King Magnus, by composing poems in honour of both kings. King Magnus gave Sturla the commission of writing his father's saga while King Hakon was out of the country on his final war cruise to the west. Sturla was in the unenviable position of having to say complimentary things about the man who had taken over his country and threatened his life. Descriptions such as *'King Hakon was not tall for a man of middle height'* may be diplomatic, but they hint at this conflict of interests. King Hakon died before the saga was complete, and Sturla escaped with his life.

King Hakon's mother, Inga, was described in the saga as *'...a good woman and faithful'*. There was still some doubt that the young Hakon was the son of the late King Hakon, so his mother offered to undertake the ordeal of bearing hot iron to prove the claim. It was believed that an innocent person could carry red hot iron in their hand without being burned, as a sign from God that they were being truthful. In 1218 Inga prepared herself to carry the iron in front of the boy king and Earl Skuli:

> There were by the king and the archbishop, the earl and other nobles of the land. There too was John earl of the Orkneys.

The ordeal was a success:

> God showed great tokens out of his mercy, so that she was well clear, and all said that who saw it that the hand was then far fairer than it was before she took hold of the iron.

Earl John, the son of Earl Harald Maddadsson, seems to have had a rocky relationship with King Hakon. As early as 1217 Earl Skuli had been secretly communicating with King Hakon's enemies. In *Hakon's Saga* we are told that:

> Earl Skuli let letters be sent west across the sea to earl John in the Orkneys, and on them was the king's seal, and the king knew nothing of it, and nothing of what was in the letters.

King Hakon heard of the letters to Earl John, but Earl Skuli was able to intercept them before they fell into the king's hands. From this we may assume that Earl John was not a loyal supporter of King Hakon.

Norway was troubled by civil war, which King Hakon managed to subdue. In 1224 he was busily asserting his authority within his realm and seeing off rival claimants to the throne. The saga has this tantalising little piece of information from that same year:

> Then came Earl John of the Orkneys and made atonement to the king in those quarrels which were between them, and set his son Harald there as a hostage, and he was with the king that summer.

Whatever the dispute was about they were on good terms in 1228:

> That summer came from the west across the sea, messengers from Earl John of the Orkneys with many good offerings, which the earl sent to King Hakon. But in the autumn the king sent the earl a good longship and many other gifts.

In 1230 there was a man called Snækoll Gunnisson who claimed some estates in Orkney that Earl John Haraldsson held in his possession. Snækoll was the great-grandson of Earl Rognvald Kali, and a nephew of Earl Harald the Younger who had been killed by Earl Harald Maddadsson. At that time King Hakon had placed a steward in Orkney called Hanef the Younger, who lived there with his brothers Kolbein and Andrew, as well as a former bodyguard of King Hakon called Oliver All-ill. Snækoll pressed his claim to the Orkney estates, but the earl refused to release them. Snækoll continued to raise the matter with Earl John:

Then the earl began to answer angrily, and asked whether he would do after the pattern of his uncle Harald, and claim the Orkneys against him. "But of a surety I mean to hold my realm against thee, as my father did by thy uncle." Snækoll answers: "It is to be looked for by me, that thou wilt grant me little of the Orkneys when thou wilt not grant me those estates which I own by right of inheritance." The earl laid great enmity on Snækoll. And he so looked at it, that he thought his life was not safe from the earl. Then he went to Hanef and his brothers, and went there into following and fellowship with them.

Both Earl John and Snækoll, accompanied by their followers, spent the following autumn and winter in Thurso. Drunken brawls broke out between their followers throughout the winter. It came to a head in 1231 when Hanef heard rumours that Earl John was planning an attack. Hanef advised Kolbein and Snækoll to arm themselves and to lead their men in an attack on the earl. They had all been drinking heavily, and considered this a good plan:

As soon as they were armed they went to that lodging in which the earl lay with strife and fire, and turned their arms on those whom they met. But when the earl was aware of the strife, then he sought to get away into some cellar, and meant to hide himself there. But they got word of where he was. They ran down thither into the cellar, Snækoll, Sumarled Rolfsson, and Oliver All-ill and Rafn, and some more. Snækoll found the earl by a tun[18]; and they dealt him there and then his death-wounds. There died with the earl some men at the hand of Hanef and his men. The earl had nine wounds.

Aerial view of Cubbie Roo's Castle, Wyre – Richard Welsby

[18] A beer barrel.

The killers headed north to Orkney, taking refuge in Cubbie Roo's castle in Wyre. They gathered stores of food together, and a herd of cattle which they kept within the ramparts of the castle defences. News of the event soon reached the islands, as well as the whereabouts of the guilty party:

> But when the friends of the earl in the Orkneys heard that, they gathered a great force, and went out into Wyre, and beleaguered the castle. But it was a very unhandy place to attack.

Kolbein of Rendall, a kinsman of Hanef, and other friends brought a truce between the two sides that would last that winter. They were to sail to Norway the following summer and submit the crime to King Hakon for his judgement:

> In the spring after they sailed to Norway, Hanef and his companions, but on board another ship sailed the earl's kinsmen and friends, and near all the best men out of the Orkneys.

They arrived in Bergen, where Hanef, Kolbein and the two brothers Sumarled and Andrew Rolfsson were imprisoned. Oliver All-ill, Thorkell the Black, Rafn and two others who were at the killing were seized and taken to a holm[19] by their Orcadian enemies and beheaded. Hanef,

'The Swelkie' - a whirlpool in the Pentland Firth where the Orkneyingars' ship was lost – Keith Allardyce

[19] A small island.

Kolbein and Snækoll went north to Trondheim with Earl Skuli and escaped punishment. The saga records a disaster for the earl of Orkney's bloodline:

> That same autumn the Orkneyingars[20] fared west and all went in one ship, the best men of the Isles. That ship was lost, and all who were in her. And many men have had to atone for this later.

Earl John's son Harald, who was a hostage in Norway, had drowned in 1226, so the loss of this ship brought an end to the Norse earls of Orkney. It now passed on through an unknown connection to Earl Magnus of the house of Angus, the first of the Scottish earls. They may have been the descendants of a granddaughter of Earl Rognvald Kali Kolsson, but this has never been proved.

Earl Skuli was later given the title of Duke, but in 1239 he had himself proclaimed king and went to war against his son-in-law, King Hakon. Skuli was killed in battle the following year, leaving Hakon the sole ruler of Norway. He was determined to bring Iceland and Greenland under his control and to reign over them as king. The saga writer Snorri Sturluson was also a politician, and he had opposed the king's claim to Iceland. King Hakon had ordered him to come to Norway, but he ignored the summons. King Hakon sent a letter to Snorri's estranged son-in-law, Gizur Thorvaldsson, that he was to bring Snorri to Norway by whatever means, or kill him in the process. Gizur attacked Snorri at his home at Reykholt on 23rd September 1241 and killed him. King Hakon would eventually gain the possession of Iceland in 1262, but he wouldn't live long to enjoy it.

King Hakon still claimed sovereignty over Orkney, Shetland and the Hebrides, which led to political tension between Scotland and Norway. King Alexander II of Scotland sent two bishops to King Hakon in 1242 to ask him to give up the Hebrides, but Hakon refused:

> And when the messengers heard this decision, they then said that the Scot-king wished to buy all the Southern Isles[21] from King Hakon, and bade him value them in burnt silver. King Hakon answers thus, that he did not know he was so much in want of silver that he needed to sell lands for it. With that the messengers went their way.

King Alexander II kept up the claim, but King Hakon refused to discuss it.

In 1248 King Hakon married his daughter, Cecilia, to Harald, whom the saga refers to as *'the Southern Isles king'*. He ruled the Hebrides from the Isle of Man, which was considered to be a part of the island group. They sailed to the Hebrides that autumn, but the ship never reached its destination. It was believed to have been lost south of Shetland, probably in the Sumburgh Roost. King Hakon had given John Duncansson the title of king that summer, and he was sent to the Hebrides to rule in place of Harald. King Alexander II took the opportunity to try to

---

[20] Orkney islanders.

[21] Viewed from Scandinavia and Orkney, the Hebrides were called the *Sudreys*, the Southern Islands, just as Sutherland got its name, the Southern Land, from this northerly vantage point.

persuade King John to give up four strategic castles and the realm that King Hakon had given him in return for land in Scotland. King John refused, remaining loyal to King Hakon. King Alexander prepared to lead an invasion of the Hebrides, and was with his forces at Kerrara near Oban.

As they lay in Kerrara, King Alexander had a dream that three men visited him:

> One seemed to him to be dressed in royal robes. That man was very unfriendly, and ruddy of face and rather thick-set, and a man of middle height. The second seemed to him slim-built, and young. Of all men the fairest, and nobly dressed. The third was by far the tallest and the most unfriendly looking of men; he was very bald on the forehead.

This last man warned him to give up his ambitions of owning the islands. The next day he told of his dream, and it was thought that the three men were St Olaf, St Magnus and St Columba respectively. This seems to have been the popular image of St Magnus, as we can see from later church altarpieces. He is depicted as a beautiful young man, beardless, and with flowing blonde curls. Despite his almost effeminate appearance he is depicted wearing a full suit of armour and holding a sword, representing a defender of the faith. Not long after having this dream King Alexander II died. He was succeeded by his son, King Alexander III, but the claim to the Hebrides didn't die with the old king.

Detail of Statuette of St Magnus in the Orkney Museum, Kirkwall – Orkney Library & Archive

In 1262 the Scots began raiding in the Hebrides, attacking Skye and causing great destruction:

> ...they fared out into Skye, and burned farms and churches, and slew a host of men and women. And they said this, that the Scots had taken small bairns and spitted them on their spear-points, and shaken them till they fell down on their hands, and cast them dead from off them.

When King Hakon (now known as Hakon the Old) heard of this slaughter he decided that he himself would lead an army west overseas to defend his territory. His son, King Magnus, offered to accompany him, but Hakon refused. He sent John Longlifsson and Henry Scot to Shetland to hire pilots to guide his battle-fleet. They continued south to Orkney, where one of the Hebridean rulers, King Dougal, was living in exile. The rumour was that King Alexander III was going to attack the islands that summer, but Dougal put out the word that King Hakon was about to sail with forty warships, which discouraged the Scots. King Hakon gathered together all the best fighting men to man his ships, including Earl Magnus of Orkney, who had joined the king in Bergen and was in command of a longship given to him by the king. This Earl Magnus was the son of Earl Gilbride and the grandson of Earl Magnus, who was the first of the Scottish earls of Orkney who inherited the earldom after the death of Earl John Haraldsson. They sailed west to Shetland, anchoring in Bressay Sound:

> King Hakon lay in Bressey sound near half a month, and sailed thence to the Orkneys, and lay in Ellidar-wick, that is near Kirkwall.

The great battle fleet anchored in Elwick Bay in Shapinsay. From there they sailed to South Ronaldsay, where they anchored for a while in *'Rognvaldsvoe'* (St Margaret's Hope). Caithness submitted to King Hakon, accepting fines rather than having to fight his army. While he was in South Ronaldsay, King Hakon heard that King John of the Hebrides had joined forces with the Scottish king. There was also a foreboding of trouble ahead:

> When King Hakon lay in Rognvaldsvoe a great darkness came over the sun, so that a little ring was bright around it on the outside, and that lasted a while of the day.

This solar eclipse can be dated to 5th August 1263.[22] Orkney men brought more ships to his force, but Earl Magnus did not join him on the expedition. The battle fleet sailed west through the Pentland Firth and then south to the Hebrides, where King Hakon was joined in Skye by King Dougal. King Hakon's fleet now comprised 120 ships, mostly large vessels, including the king's own ship, the *Krossuden* (Cross-clinker), which was decorated with a golden dragon's head. This ship had thirty seven pairs of oars, and could carry around 300 men.

---

[22] Thomson, William P.L., *The New History of Orkney.* Mecat Press, Edinburgh, 2001. 142.

King Hakon's fleet lay at Kerrera, while some of the ships went raiding in Scotland. Many areas surrendered to the king, who had given orders that churches should be spared. King John had come to see King Hakon, saying that he had been given a large estate in Scotland in return for his support and had sworn oaths to the Scottish King. Hakon kept him with him for a while and treated him well. Messages arrived from Ireland requesting King Hakon's help to defeat the English, who had taken over the best coastal towns in the country. In return they had offered to accept him as their king. King Hakon sent a small ship to Ireland to discover what the Irish were actually offering, and at what cost to himself.

Messengers also arrived from the Scottish king asking for peace. King Hakon had expected this, and he sent his negotiators Bishop Gilbert of Hamar and Bishop Henry of Orkney. King John and other powerful men went with them to try to bring about peace between the two kings. King Alexander III gave the impression that he wanted peace, but he delayed his decision in the hope that the weather would break, as it was already September. King Hakon suspected that the Scots were just playing for time, and he sent a message to the Scottish king saying that they should meet in person with a band of their best warriors, and if peace terms could not be reached, then they would fight. Again King Alexander III gave little away as to what he intended to do. King Hakon declared that the truce was now over, and the Norsemen began raiding in Scotland.

By the beginning of October the weather broke, just as the Scottish king had hoped, and gales lashed King Hakon's fleet. It took eight anchors to hold the king's ship, while five other ships were driven ashore. It was hardly surprising that they should encounter a gale in Scotland at that time of the year, but they considered it more than just bad luck:

> Most men so spoke that witchcraft must have brought about this storm.

Two of the ships had been re-floated, but three remained stranded. The Scots came down and shot at the Norsemen, causing injuries but few deaths.

The following day, 2nd October 1263, King Hakon went ashore with many men. The Scots had gathered a great force together, and moved to attack the Norsemen. With some difficulty they persuaded King Hakon to return to his ship while the Norsemen gathered as many men as they could get from the ships in order to fight. The Battle of Largs, as it became known, was an indecisive and somewhat scrappy fight, in which the heavily outnumbered Norse army held their own against the Scots throughout the day. The Norsemen were fighting during a gale, so many of the men on the ships couldn't land. After one last push the Scots fell back, allowing the remaining Norsemen to escape in boats back to their longships. The Scottish army retreated inland, allowing the Norsemen to recover the bodies of the slain for burial. Although the battle was not the huge victory that the Scots had wanted, it was the beginning of the end of Norse rule in the Hebrides. King Hakon's expedition had changed nothing, and the Scottish king's position was stronger than ever.

Word was brought to King Hakon that the Irish were offering to provide food and shelter for his army over the coming winter if he would fight the English for them. King Hakon was keen to take up the offer, but his men wanted to return home. At the end of October the fleet returned to Orkney and many of his men returned home to Norway. King Hakon had decided to stay the winter in Orkney:

> Then he named near twenty ships to stay behind, but to the others he gave leave to sail home.

The ships were beached at Scapa Bay and Houton, by the shores of Scapa Flow.

By this time the king was suffering from ill-health, a major factor in his decision to spend the winter in Orkney:

> He was there very sick that night he was on board ship. Next morning he let mass be sung for him on land. After that he settled about his ship, where she should be laid up, and bade men to bestow great pains in caring for the ship. After that he fared into Scapa-neck,[23] and so to Kirkwall; he went to the bishop's house with all his train for whom he kept table. They both had their boards in the hall, the king and the bishop, each of them for his men; but the king was up in his lodging, and took his meat always there.

Detail of stone carvings within St Magnus Cathedral, Kirkwall – Raymond Parks

[23] Scapa Bay.

The king's illness slowly worsened so that he was in bed for three weeks. After that he seemed to improve, as his saga records:

> ...for some three days he was in that state that he walked the first day much about his lodging, and the next into the bishop's chapel, and heard mass there; but the third day he walked to St Magnus' church, and round the shrine of Saint Magnus the earl.

He felt well enough to have a bath and a shave, but it all proved to be too much for him. The sickness returned, and he was forced to take to his bed once more. He probably turned to the library of St Magnus Cathedral for relief from the boredom of lying in bed:

> In the sickness he let Latin books be read to him at first. But then he thought it great trouble to think over what that (the Latin) meant. Then he let be read to him Norse books, night and day; first the Sagas of the saints; and when they were read out he let be read to him the tales of the kings from Halfdan the Black, and so on of all the kings of Norway, one after the other.

The stone marking the temporary burial place of King Hakon Hakonsson, within St Rognvald's Chapel, St Magnus Cathedral, Kirkwall – Orkney Library & Archive

It is ironic to think that the old man lying on his deathbed listening to Snorri Sturluson's *Heimskringla* was the same person who ordered his murder twenty-two years previously.

As the king's condition worsened, he ordered his goods to be split up between his followers, and he had letters sent to his son, King Magnus. He also swore that he had no other children than King Magnus and his daughters, in case there were any pretenders to the throne:

> When the tale of the kings was read down to Sverri, then he let them take to reading Sverri's Saga. Then it was read both night and day whenever he was awake. The mass-day of St Lucy the virgin was on a Thursday.[24] But the Saturday after, late in the evening, the course of the king's sickness was so heavy on him that he lost his speech. Near midnight Sverri's Saga was read through. But just as midnight was past Almighty God called King Hakon from this world's life.

The king's body was washed and he was shaved and dressed in fine robes and a garland was placed on his head. On the Sunday it was carried up to the 'upper hall' where it was placed on a bier for his followers to see. Mass was sung for his soul in the hall, which was lit by *'candle-swains'* bearing torches and was watched over by his faithful bodyguards. On the Monday his body was carried to St Magnus Cathedral where his guards again watched over him. King Hakon was placed in his coffin and buried on the Tuesday with much pomp and ceremony:

> He was buried in the choir in Magnus' church there on the steps before the shrine of Saint Magnus the earl.

His bodyguards held a vigil over his grave until the following March, when King Hakon's body was exhumed and carried to Bergen to lie alongside his ancestors. A stone marks the spot in the cathedral where King Hakon the Old's body lay over the winter of 1263–64.

Hakon's son, King Magnus, bowed to the inevitable and sold the Hebrides to Scotland in 1266. Four thousand marks were to be paid over four years, with an annual payment of 100 marks thereafter. This payment was to take place in St Magnus Cathedral, overseen by the bishop of Orkney or the king's officials. Norway was losing its grip on its territories west over the sea. Orkney would be lost in 1468, and Shetland the following year. Although the Northern Isles have been a part of Scotland now for some 550 years at the time that this book was written, the culture, folklore and language retain much of its Viking ancestry. Orcadians and Shetlanders to this day still take a great pride in the fact that we have our own place among the Icelandic Sagas.

---

[24] 15th December.

COMBS

Given their frequent occurrence as archaeological finds, hair combs seem to have been common objects right across Europe during the Viking Age. Indeed, they have a long history, with prehistoric and Roman examples also widespread. The making of combs was a slow, arduous, and highly skilled task. First, a number of small toothplates would be cut from a large mammal bone, or more commonly from deer antler, and these would then be riveted together between two much longer connecting plates made of bone or antler. Decoration was often elaborate, so the construction of a single comb probably took the best part of a day to complete.

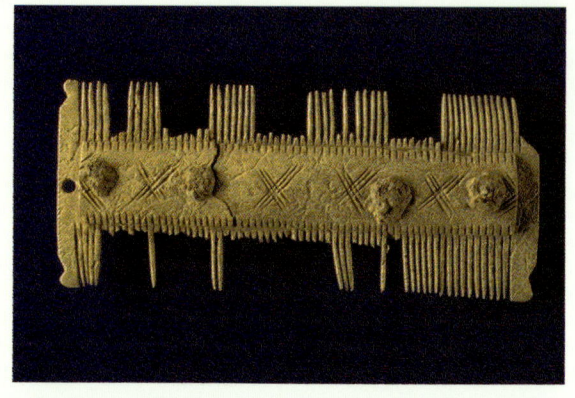

Double-sided high-backed comb from Skaill, Deerness – Orkney Museums and Heritage

In Orkney, combs seem to have become really popular in the Pictish period, and a range of highly decorative single- and double-sided combs are known from this time. Viking Age combs have a very different design, and it is at this point in time that combs from Orkney and other parts of Europe start to look alike; for example, the second comb pictured is very similar to examples known from the site of Birka, in southern Sweden[1]. This means that combs from the Viking Age are quite easily recognised. Interestingly, Pictish and Viking Age combs are mixed together at some Orcadian sites, perhaps suggesting that relations between the two groups were not always hostile[2]. However, it is important to note that no-one is really sure *who* was using which sort of comb.

There are a few documentary references to the use of combs; in *Laxdaela Saga* Unn the Deep-minded loses her comb at a place thereafter referred to as Kambsness, while *Heimskringla* recounts the famous story of the Norse king Harald, who declared that he would not comb or trim his hair until he had subdued the whole of Norway. Upon successful completion of this mission, he became known as Harald Finehair. These references only give us a glimpse of how combs were used, but they do suggest that they were commonly recognised objects. It is clear that they were used in personal grooming, though the coarse gauge of many early examples would have limited their effectiveness in the removal of nits and lice.

However, it is unlikely that the use of Pictish and Viking Age combs was limited to personal hygiene, given the long and complicated manufacturing process and often painstaking decoration involved. A number of examples are equipped with decorative cases, while others sport holes that might suggest that some form of thong was used to suspend them, either from the waist or the neck, or perhaps from a nail in the wall. Thus, it may be appropriate to view such combs as dress accessories with an important role in display.

Combs may also have had some sort of symbolic significance, as they occur frequently on the Pictish symbol stones[3]. By the Viking Age, their meaning may have changed, but very large, ornate combs suggest that they were still considered important. It is also notable that combs are one of the more common finds in Viking Age graves. Combs were reported at several of the graves from the cemetery near Pierowall, in Westray [4], and they are also

High-backed Pictish comb from Buckquoy, Birsay – Orkney Museums and Heritage

Norse comb from Deerness made of antler with copper alloy rivets. *c*. thirteenth-century – Orkney Museums and Heritage

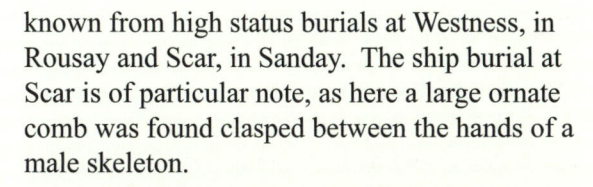

known from high status burials at Westness, in Rousay and Scar, in Sanday. The ship burial at Scar is of particular note, as here a large ornate comb was found clasped between the hands of a male skeleton.

However, by the time of the Icelandic sagas, Orkney may be seen to have been largely Christianised, and Christian burials rarely contain grave goods. Furthermore, very large combs become rare, with the majority of examples from the tenth/eleventh century onward being smaller and more simply decorated. Perhaps there was a move away from ostentatious objects for display or exchange of gifts, and towards functional simplicity. However, while in England this trend continues until well after the Norman Conquest, the Northern Isles see a variety of unusual types. An important development is the use of rivets as an active component of decoration. Indeed, one comb from the Brough of Birsay uses rolls of copper alloy sheet, rather than solid pegs[5].

Some such combs are just as large and flamboyant as their early Viking Age ancestors; the best example of this is an extremely long comb from the high status site at Skaill, in Deerness. It has even been suggested that some types were fashioned to look like fish[6]. The closest parallels for many of these types lie in Scandinavia, which fits well with Orkney's continued political and cultural association with Norway.

Thus, for a considerable period of Orkney's later prehistory and early history, hair combs seem to have been important personal possessions. Nonetheless, they seem to have been fairly common, everyday objects, and this, together with the tough materials from which they were made, means that archaeologists find them very useful. This is because their changes, due to fashion, mean that they can be used to date settlements, rubbish dumps, and graves, and differences in design between regions can be used to help understand trade, politics, and contact between peoples.

Steven P Ashby

References/ Further Reading

Ambrosiani, K. 1981: *Viking Age Combs, Comb Making and Comb Makers in the Light of Finds from Birka and Ribe*, Stockholm: Stockholm Studies in Archaeology 2.

Arbman, H. 1943: *Birka I, Die Gräber*, Stockholm: Text, KVHAA.

Buteux, S. (ed.) 1997: *Settlements at Skaill, Deerness, Orkney: Excavations by Peter Gelling of the Prehistoric, Pictish, Viking and Later Periods, 1963-1981*, Oxford: British Archaeological Reports, British Series 260.

Clarke, D. and Heald, A. 2002: Beyond typology: combs, economics, symbolism and regional identity in Late Norse Scotland, *Norwegian Archaeological Review* 35: 81-93.

Crawford, I. A. 1981: 'War or Peace - Viking Colonisation in the Northern and Western Isles of Scotland Reviewed', In Proceedings of the Eighth Viking Congress, Århus 1977, Medieval Scandinavia Supplements Volume 2, Odense: , Odense University Press, pp.259-269.

Cummins, W. A. 1999: *The Picts and Their Symbols*, Stroud: Sutton.

Curle, C. L. 1982: *Pictish and Norse Finds from the Brough of Birsay 1934-74*, Edinburgh: Society of Antiquaries of Scotland Monograph Series Number 1.

Owen, O. and Dalland, M. 1999: *Scar: A Viking Boat Burial on Sanday, Orkney*, Phantassie, Scotland: Tuckwell Press.

Thorsteinsson, A. 1968: 'The Viking Burial Place at Pierowall, Westray, Orkney', In B. Niclasen(ed.) The Fifth Viking Congress: Tórshavn, July 1965, Tórshavn: Føroya Landsstyri, pp.150-173.

Early Norse bone comb from the Brough of Birsay – Orkney Museums and Heritage

Viking comb made of antler with iron rivets from the boat burial at Scar, Sanday – Orkney Museums and Heritage

[1] Arbman 1943; Ambrosiani 1981

[2] Crawford 1981; Curle 1982; Buteux 1997

[3] Cummins 1999

[4] Thorsteinsson 1968

[5] Curle 1982

[6] Clarke and Heald 2002

Interior Bishop's Palace, Kirkwall – Raymond Parks

RUNES

The first runic alphabet probably originated just after the birth of Christianity. There were twenty-four phonetic symbols, and, with some minor variations, these were common to all the Germanic peoples who used runes.

This 'Futhark,' named for its first six letters which represent the sounds

'f' 'u' 'th' 'a' 'r' 'k'

was used to represent Old Norse, as spoken by Scandinavian people until about the year 700.

The alphabet and the runes were evolving, however, and the futhark of the Viking Age proper, c. 700-1050, only contained sixteen runes. This reduction meant that one rune must now represent more than one sound. The problems caused by this led to the addition of three dotted runes (stungne) during the eleventh century.

It is not clear where and how runes originated. It is obvious that Latin capitals led to about a third of the alphabet, but scholars have suggested other influences, including Greek, Etruscan, north Italian, Celts, Goths, Marcomanni and Eruli. It is generally concluded that the futhark came in part from one or more southern European alphabets, and that it was in part invented. The use of vertical and diagonal strokes in the main suggested that it was designed for use on wood, and runes have been found in Orkney on stone and on animal bone.

Many scholars mention the magical significance of runes, and they were certainly used for spells and magic. Increasingly, however, they were used for other more day-to-day purposes, such as recording events, and identifying people and places.

Steve Callaghan

The reconstructed longhouse at Stong, Iceland – based on the house of Gauk Trindilsson, who is mentioned by name in the runic inscriptions in Maeshowe. 'These runes were carved by the man most skilled in runes in the Western Ocean' and 'with this axe owned by Gauk Trindilsson in the South land' (of Iceland). The captain of the ship that brought Earl Rognvald back to Orkney after his crusade was Thorhall Asgrimsson, the great-great-great-grandson of the man who killed Gauk
– Ásborg Arnþórsdóttir.

Runes on cow rib bone found at Bu, Orphir, Orkney
– Orkney Library & Archive

Viking graffiti – runes carved by Vikings who broke into the Neolithic tomb of Maeshowe in Orkney. This is the most extensive group of runic inscriptions found outside Scandinavia.
– Agne Säterberg

The rune stone found in the church at Bu, Orphir, Orkney – Orkney Library & Archive

Reference and further reading:

Jones, G J, 1984, A History of the Vikings, Oxford University Press, Oxford.

Round Kirk, Orphir – Raymond Parks

SAGA TRANSLATIONS USED IN THIS BOOK

Edda, (Snorri Sturluson), Anthony Faulks, Everyman, London, 2001.

Flatyjarbók, Sir George W. Dasent, 1894 (appendix to his translation of the *Orkneyinga Saga*).

Færeyinga Saga (The Saga of the Faeroe Islanders), F. York Powell, 1896, (reprinted by Llanerch Publishers, Wales, 1995).

Hakonar Saga (The Saga of King Hacon), Sir George W. Dasent, 1894 (reprinted by Llanerch Publishers, Wales, 1997).

Heimskringla (The Sagas of the Kings of Norway) (Snorri Sturluson) Erling Monsen (assisted by A.H. Smith), Dover Publishing, New York, 1990.

Historie Norwegie (History of Norway), Peter Fisher, Mareum Tusculanum Press, Copenhagen, 2003.

Landnamabók (The Book of Settlements), Hermann Pálsson and Paul Edwards, Manitoba, 1972.

The Longer Magnus Saga, Sir George W. Dasent, 1894 (appendix to his translation of the *Orkneyinga Saga*).

Orkneyinga Saga (The Saga of the Orkney Islanders) A.B. Taylor, Oliver and Boyd, Edinburgh, 1938.

The Saga of the Volsungs, Jesse L. Byock, Penguin Books, London, 1999.

Sverri's Saga (The Saga of King Sverri), J. Sephton, 1899 (reprinted by Llanerch Publishers, Wales, 1994).

TRANSLATIONS USED FROM THE FIVE VOLUME SET 'THE COMPLETE SAGAS OF ICELANDERS'
Leifur Eiríksson Publishing
Reykjavik, 1997.

Brennu-Njáls Saga (Njal's Saga), Robert Cook.

Egils Saga Skallagrímssonar (Egil's Saga), Bernard Scudder.

Eyrbyggja Saga (The Saga of the People of Eyri), Judy Quinn.

Gunnlaugs Saga Ormstunga (The Saga of Gunnlaug Serpent-Tongue), Katrina C. Attwood.

Laxdæla Saga (The Saga of the People of Laxerdal), Keneva Kunz.

Þorstein's Saga Síðu-Hallssonar (Thorstein Sidu-Hallsson's Saga), Katrina C. Attwood.

Vatnsdæla Saga (The Saga of the People of Vatnsdal), Andrew Wawn.

Map of Orkney in modern times

- North Ronaldsay
- Papa Westray
- Westray
- Sanday
- Faray
- Rousay
- Egilsay
- Eday
- Papa Stronsay
- Eynhallow
- Stronsay
- Brough of Birsay
- BIRSAY
- EVIE
- Wyre
- SANDWICK
- Dounby
- RENDALL
- Gairsay
- Auskerry
- Shapinsay
- FIRTH
- Damsay
- Loch of Harray
- Finstown
- Loch of Stenness
- STENNESS
- KIRKWALL
- TANKERNESS
- STROMNESS
- DEERNESS
- Graemsay
- ORPHIR
- SCAPA FLOW
- Copinsay
- Cava
- Hoy
- Burray
- Fara
- Flotta
- Longhope
- South Ronaldsay
- Swona

PENTLAND FIRTH

John O' Groats

CAITHNESS